INTELLIGENT SPACES

ARCHITECTURE FOR THE INFORMATION AGE

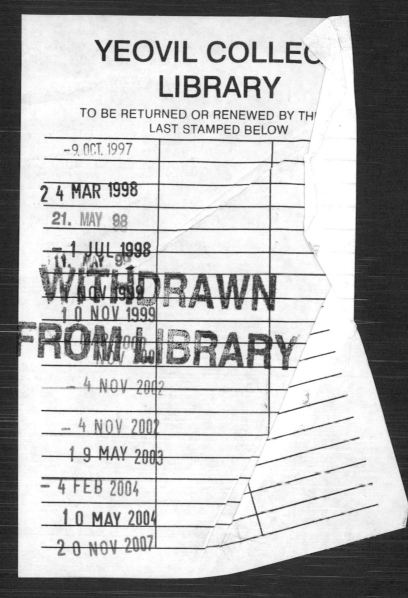

INTELLIGENT SPACES

ARCHITECTURE FOR THE INFORMATION AGE

OTTO RIEWOLDT
CO-ORDINATING RESEARCHER: JENNIFER HUDSON

LAURENCE KING

Published 1997 by Laurence King Publishing
an imprint of Calmann & King Ltd
71 Great Russell Street, London WC1B 3BN

A catalogue record for this book is available from the British
Library.

ISBN 1 85669 097 0

Translated from the German by Susan Mackervoy
Designed by Mikhail and Helen Anikst

Printed in Hong Kong

The author, the co-ordinating researcher and the
publishers would like to thank John Taylor
for his kind and patient co-operation in editing this book;
Yasuyuki Hirai for his dedicated research for Japanese
projects; all the architects and designers who contributed
to the projects; the photographers whose work
has been reproduced; and the various companies
and corporations that supplied additional information
on projects featured.

CONTENTS

As the twentieth century draws to a close the media revolution is becoming a tangible, compelling reality. Data highways span the globe, worldwide electronic networks are transforming the economy, information systems and the entertainment industry. Computer and television technologies are merging to create on-line multimedia services, the goldmines of the future. These dynamic new markets are producing a wide range of responses from architects and interior designers: professional users and private clients want more than just the latest technology – they also want an appropriate architectural setting. A building which reflects (or appears to reflect) this market context can be a key factor in promoting a company and enhancing its image. Architecture and design have their own special role to play in the new Information Age: creating the promising, visual setting that provides a foretaste of the virtual delights housed within.

Yet this simple description conceals a fundamental paradox. The borderlessness of the technological world is thoroughly at odds with the containing structures of buildings: virtual reality by its very essence has less and less need for architecture, finally making it obsolete, redundant. The digital revolution is based on simultaneity, synchronicity, permanence, immateriality, immediacy and globality. The virtual image, a medium for electronic information, communication and entertainment, is accessible anywhere and located nowhere. Its users, whether they be employees, customers or leisure-surfers, are dispersed and isolated, connected only by modem to the electronic web of Internet and Intranets. What they see and experience is no mere illustration or simulation of reality, but a new immaterial reality of its own kind. All their interactions, transactions and work processes take place in the everywhere and nowhere of the Net. The qualitative revolution in multimedia technology is now turning into a quantitative revolution: in 1995, revenues from data services on the US telephone networks exceeded revenues from ordinary telephone usage for the first time.

This move towards digital civilization involves more than just the partial eclipse of our text-based culture by the image. In the words of French philosopher Paul Virilio: "Speed burns up space. With telecommunications the modern age has reached absolute speed. Everything is live, direct – in real time." The conquest of time and distance at once perfects individual mobility and makes it redundant. There is no longer any need to travel: the world will come to you, and everything happens on the computer screen.

The real design innovations of the Information Age relate to the presentation of electronic data. Architecture has become an anachronism, if not superfluous then certainly problematic, as Dutch architect Rem Koolhaas sarcastically observed in his theoretical article "S, M, L, XL" of 1995: "Our amalgamated wisdom can be caricatured: according to Derrida we cannot be Whole, according to Baudrillard we cannot be Real, according to Virilio we cannot be There – inconvenient repertoire for a profession helplessly about being Whole, Real and There." In these circumstances the present volume cannot claim to be more than a stocktaking exercise. The case studies presented here do not form part of a cohesive new architectural trend – rather they are widely varying responses to the challenge of the electronic age. The fact that the geographic balance is heavily weighted towards the USA and Japan is no coincidence: it is in these countries that the multimedia revolution has had its strongest technical and economic impact.

The starting point was a series of questions: How is architecture responding in places where the new technologies are used professionally? What kind of architectural corporate identity is being developed by companies in the multimedia industry (Chapter 1)? How are electronically networked office worlds being redefined (Chapter 2)? How is computerization changing the programmes and constructional features of multi-functional projects (Chapter 3)? How are the new information and entertainment centres, which are packed with multimedia equipment and interactive computer simulations, and which are usually overlooked by theorists commenting on the architectural scene, coping with the challenge (Chapter 4)? How is the influx of electronic storage media and data networks affecting cultural and educational institutions (Chapter 5)?

For all the diversity of individual architectural solutions, three general trends can be observed, affecting the form, function and construction of buildings. In formal terms, architects are exploiting the futuristic potential contained within the buildings, turning actuality and progressiveness into stylistic features. The new virtual reality is imitated and adapted in the architecture, with science-fiction, imaginative backdrops and an expressive range which extends from cartoon-inspired fun architecture to deconstructivist designs which continue postmodernist preoccupations in a relaxed, eclectic fashion. Reductionist architecture, including high-tech and improvised workshop styles, might appear at first sight to be the polar opposite to this expressive architectural trend: in fact it can be seen as an alternative, parallel response to the same problem. By reacting to the digital dematerialization of the world, architecture becomes increasingly individualized: in the words of American architectural critic Herbert Muschamp, "subjectivity takes command. Like surrealists these architects seem determined to blur the border between waking reality and the dream state."

The dynamic multimedia industry is undergoing rapid change, with global mega-mergers and record-breaking stock-market flotations: companies in this sector are looking for architectural settings which convey and enhance a corporate image. This is especially true of those projects that are directly targeted at the public. For all the euphoria about lucrative new forms of commercialization such as home-shopping, telebanking, pay-television, and video-on-demand, direct interaction in urban architectural settings is set to remain a core element of the business world. Cybertainment as a collective experience is still at an early stage of development. Concepts like Segaworld or The Edge

by US theme-park operator Landmark are to be set up in dozens of cities worldwide over the next few years; in the USA, and probably soon elsewhere, there is to be a chain of new Sony cinema centres which will transform the traditional multiplex into digital pleasure domes.

In terms of architectural functions, the current trend is towards mixed-function buildings, hybrid constructions combining under a single roof functions which had previously been separated. This process of concentration and interpenetration is taking place across the scale: from the urbanization of individual buildings, to the development of new urban mega-structures. Rem Koolhaas created the most radical example of this architectural type with the gigantic Eurolille project in the French city of Lille; he refers enthusiastically to "contamination through the overlapping of functions" and the "alchemy of mixed uses". This escape from the strict categorizations of architecture and town-planning is made possible – indeed inevitable – by the digital revolution. "Cyberspace means the end of that central institutional paradigm of modern life, the bureaucratic organization", proclaimed *Cyberspace and the American Dream*, a manifesto book published in the USA in 1994. The on-line computer is no longer just an administrative tool, it has become a multiple medium for information and communication. The work processes and structures of today's companies are becoming increasingly virtual: they exist and function through software and the Internet rather than the rational and hierarchical structures of an architectural environment. Hyperlinks have superseded spatial relations.

The decline of traditional bureaucracy is redefining the workplace. Employees are becoming office nomads: in the branches of American advertising agency Chiat/Day, laptop trolleys and sockets await the company's vagabond workers. Today, the computer giant IBM still has a fixed desk space for one in two of its workers; in the future the company plans to accommodate only 20 per cent of its workforce in company offices. The software company SAP is globalizing its research and development work: teams in Europe, the USA and Japan collaborate on cooperative projects simultaneously, passing the project on to the next global think-tank at the end of each working day. Andersen Consulting set a leading example for many other companies and agencies by using the accumulated know-how of all its consulting projects to set up a database which is continuously updated and made available to its 29,000 consultants worldwide.

The global enterprise of the future will be a composite, changing network of autonomous units. On an individual level, software potentate Bill Gates and the experts of America's MIT Medialab are predicting the total computerization of living environments: "things that think" will provide integrated, "smart" systems controlling all domestic functions. Private and professional spheres will finally begin to merge in this digital paradise. At least, this is how leading Hollywood figures Steven Spielberg, Jeffrey Katzenberg and David Geffen see the future. Their company SKG Dreamworks is planning a new type of utopia. On the site of Howard Hughes' former aircraft factories they are going to create Playa Vista, a $200 million "prototype of a twenty-first-century community", a joint venture with industrial partners including GTE, IBM and Silicon Graphics. The studio complex will be surrounded by a multimedia commercial park with private houses: and it will be car-free.

In constructional terms, architecture in the Information Age is finally realizing what the founders of cybernetics anticipated in their theories fifty years ago. At that time cybernetics pioneer Norbert Wiener was looking for analogies between technical and organic regulation and communication systems, and formulated a new theory of automation. Today, intelligent buildings are evolving into self-regulating machines which can adapt their internal conditions to suit changing environmental factors. "Technology has become the companion of tectonics", observes German architecture critic Manfred Sack, with justice. Computers control the whole range of building technology functions, including climate, heating, sun-protection and lighting, minimizing energy consumption and enhancing the building's economic, ergonomic and ecological profiles. In some cases the building becomes self-sufficient, as solar cells on the walls or the roof provide some of the energy it needs. As buildings evolve into a sensitive interface between their interior space and the external environment, so the nature of the building's outer layer is changing. It is becoming a skin, which is developing new technical and aesthetic qualities. The new head office of the Commerzbank in Frankfurt, currently under construction, offers a prototype of how eco-centric innovation will affect the large-scale projects of the future. Norman Foster's design is an impressive high-tech tower: yet it is more than this; it is also a complex, self-regulating biosphere, with internal courtyards full of hanging gardens, and a high level of energy efficiency.

A closer consideration of contemporary architecture reveals that these trends – formal, functional and constructional – cannot be entirely disentangled. In many projects they overlap and intersect. The avant-garde of the 1960s and 1970s hoped that the media revolution would act as a spur to architectural progress; the propagandists of the newly discovered Light Architecture firmly believe that this is happening. In his preface to the Light Architecture exhibition in the New York Museum of Modern Art in 1995, Terence Riley mused: "It is not surprising that the pervasive presence in contemporary culture of film, television, video, computer screens representing a unique sensibility of light, movement and information, should find its way into architecture". The present overview does not offer any conclusive proof that the media revolution and architectural progress are necessarily connected. Architects may dream of the media-building, in their desire to dematerialize architecture by borrowing from the new technologies. However, it is no coincidence that ambitious plans by Jean Nouvel and others to make houses and streets into living picture screens have not got beyond the drawing board. Instead, the leading entertainment companies are preparing to take over whole areas of the world's cities. By the turn of the century the Disney group will have transformed a desolate corner at the heart of Manhattan into a perfect fake Toontown. It is the theme parks' camouflage of the entertainment industry rather than the computerized media that are taking over the urban landscape.

Experimental architects like Bernard Tschumi still base their work on the assumption that architecture is directly influenced by technological developments: "The appearance of permanence (buildings are solid; they are made of steel, concrete, bricks, etc.) is increasingly challenged by the immaterial representation of abstract systems (television and electronic images)". However, in reality the reverse seems true. Innovative designs show a clear preference for glass, metal and new composite materials: but this can be attributed to the high flexibility of these materials and does not necessarily indicate a new media-based architecture. The dual theme of transparency and concealment, of opening and containment, has been heralded by some as a modern-day leitmotif: in fact it is based on age-old architectural principles. The unity of content and form, or indeed between function and construction, is beginning to break down as the digital revolution leaves architecture to its own devices. Computer networks and workstations can function in the most diverse of contexts. Computer-based building management systems may well be installed in new buildings or in protected monuments. Historical buildings are being turned into ultra-modern banking centres. Restoration, image creation and state-of-the-art communications technology can all live together. Leading scientific institutions can be housed in multicoloured wooden shacks or in high-tech research stations. Artistic improvisation or rigid structures, post-modern irony and cybernetics, high-tech as a style gesture or as hyper-functionalism: anything goes.

In practical terms, the fact that anything is possible owes much to CAD design systems. For architects the computer does indeed open up new possibilities, enabling them to calculate, depict and construct more or less any type of stylistic experiment. Complex simulation processes enable designers to modify heating and lighting systems in order to meet the desired or stipulated standards with exact precision. In this way the computer as a design tool is restoring the autonomy of architecture: as Toyo Ito observes, not without self-criticism, in the notes to his media library design for Sendai in Japan, "In the later half of the 1980s, in order to shake off the almost autistic formalism in architecture, we utilized a number of metaphors in order to emphasize the image of architecture in the information city. The focus of our interest shifted to seeing to what extent we could dissolve, or mutate the conventional program."

The paradoxical situation of architecture in the Information Age is beginning to intensify into sheer antagonism. Cyberspace is no home to live in: it threatens social cohesiveness and countless jobs. The threat of "jobless growth", the proportional growth of profit and mass unemployment, is becoming a reality. American sociologist Richard Sennet equates the overall gain in flexibility with an existential loss of security: "Work no longer provides the worker with a stable identity. Thanks to these economic changes even the workplace has lost its importance and identity." The trend towards teleworking is replacing centralized workplaces with diffused satellite or home offices. On a larger scale, companies are relocating whole operational units from high-cost sites to cheaper locations: American Express, Lufthansa and other large corporations have moved their computer and accounts centres to India. Work is emigrating to the far corners of the earth. Global sourcing has blurred the distinction between product and service, and the webs of commercial enterprise span the whole world, controlled, coordinated and networked electronically. This wave of automatization is eliminating whole layers of management, heralding the end of the administrative corporate colossus. Today, global groups like ABB are managed by scaled-down mini-holdings. Finance industries, banks and insurance companies expect to reduce their workforces by at least 20 to 30 per cent over the next few years. In this respect, to adapt Virilio's observation, digitalization is burning up space: space for working and living in. Virtual corporate structures need less office space, fewer parking spaces, and fewer facilities for the public.

For architecture this means a return to its elementary protective and identity-creating functions, to its basic role of providing accommodation, a real living environment separate from the insubstantial worlds of the computer. German architectural historian Dieter Hoffmann-Axthelm predicts the emergence of a new urbanity, answering the growing requirement for authentic experiences: "The insubstantiality of electronic networks will result in an increased emphasis on materiality, locality, borders, fixed boundaries". Viewed from this angle, the real challenge for architecture in the Information Age is to invert the relationship between purpose and means. In this context, intelligent spaces would

not be those designed for the optimal accommodation or display of multimedia technologies but those that use the opportunities provided by the new technologies to humanize living environments. Whether in front of a monitor or under a headset, cybernauts should be able to turn away from the virtual images and return to an architectural reality that re-unites them with their socio-cultural and natural environment, in aesthetic terms and, even more important, in ergonomic and ecological terms.

Digital technologies can add a new dimension to architecture, but they cannot redefine its fundamental character. For architecture, utopia will continue to lie in the real world, not the virtual realm. According to Toyo Ito, architecture can and must assert itself in the face of total computerization: "Current building types are moribund. They no longer have the strength to keep up with the realities of society and the huge scale of the digital network ocean is forcing a radical re-constitution of architectural programs."

Otto Riewoldt

1

THE MULTIMEDIA INDUSTRY

Multimedia and interactive communications services represent the growth industry of our era. Producers of hardware and software, media groups, television companies, digital studio companies, advertising agencies and traditional publishing operations: in their architectural settings all these companies are looking to the future, heralding the revolution that has already begun. The range of styles and forms encompasses sober high-tech and futuristic theatricality. There is no longer any necessary functional connection between the content of these working environments and their appearance. The electronic products are generated by decentralized, networked staff, imposing ever fewer restrictions on the architectural reality. In this context the primary role of architecture is to convey a corporate message of optimism and growth.

CHANNEL 4, LONDON, UK

ARCHITECT:
RICHARD ROGERS PARTNERSHIP
1994

Channel 4's London headquarters is a striking, dramatic construction incorporating references to industrial architecture. Yet its expressive style is deceptive: this is no futurist prelude to the electronic age but simply two well-composed, conventional office buildings, presented and joined together with panache. Production facilities and studios were not at the top of the company's list of requirements. It wanted an administrative headquarters with 15,000 square metres of office space, to be built on a plot which had been bombed during the war, next to a fairly down-market residential area in Pimlico. The building was to bring together the various branches of the television company, previously housed in locations across London, with sections which could be sublet to other users (including companies unconnected with the media).

The winning design was by Richard Rogers, the champion of high-tech architecture. His L-shaped television building takes up two sides of the rectangular site; the two other sides of the site were sold for residential development by others (these have made a significant contribution to refinancing the £38-million project). The block is designed in a persuasive urban style with an interior landscaped garden and a semi-circular piazza opening on to the street. The entrance, surrounded by galleries, presents a spectacular display of fine engineering in glass and metal. Channel 4's transmission centre, the technical heart of the building, is in the basement, along with a cinema.

In its new building this renowned television company, famous for its ambitious productions, is paving the way for interactive television and the digital technologies of the future. However, the technological revolution does not require a revolutionary architectural setting: efficient, functional offices are sufficient. It is typical of the building's stylistic sophistication that Rogers celebrates the advent of the electronic age with a nostalgic reference to the past: for the rust-red of the façade construction his co-architect John Young chose the exact colour of San Francisco's Golden Gate Bridge.

The dominant feature and centrepiece of the Channel 4 headquarters is the concave glazed entrance. This is flanked by two "satellite towers" containing conference rooms (*right*) and lifts, electrical plant and transmission antennae (*left*).

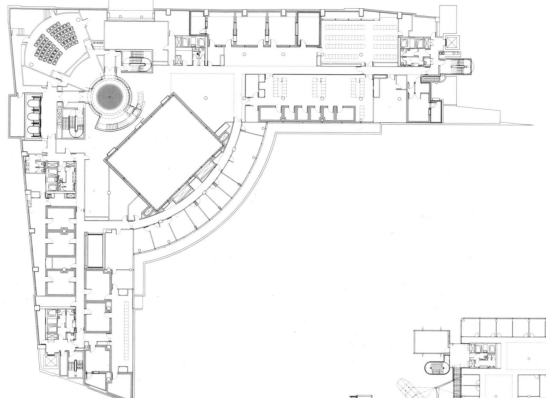

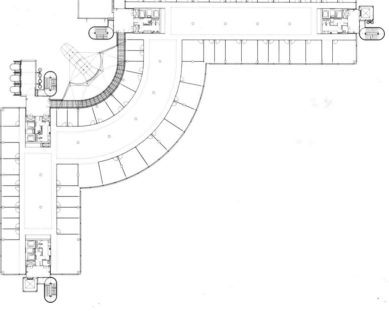

Plans of site (*below*), basement (*above*) and
ground floor (*right*) illustrate Rogers' intelligent adaptation of the corner site. The two,
four-storey office wings are arranged in an
L-shape, linked by a curved connecting space.
Residential buildings overlooking a semi-public garden will form the remaining two sides.

Opposite:
The transparency that results from the use of
plate glass, glass blocks and pewter-grey
aluminium cladding is a deliberate attempt
to reduce the impact of the building on an
already crowded urban setting. To minimize
glare and achieve high energy-efficiency
levels, light mesh screens have been added to
the lower portion of the office glazing.

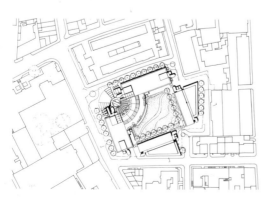

Opposite:
The atrium lobby is overlooked by three storeys of offices.

Right:
A stepped ramp leads to the entrance. Access is gained through a revolving glass door in a suspended glazed wall, and over a glass bridge which spans a rooflight to the studios below.

Below:
The design principle of transparency is maintained in the office areas, where glazed partition walls are equipped with integrated blinds.

DISNEY FEATURE ANIMATION BUILDING, BURBANK, USA

ARCHITECT:
ROBERT A.M. STERN ARCHITECTS/MORRIS ARCHITECTS
INTERIOR DESIGNER:
ROBERT A.M. STERN ARCHITECTS
1994

This fun factory is the home of the world's most successful comic figures, producing an endless stream of blockbuster cartoon films and series. Here, on an area of 25,800 square metres, 700 creative artists work at drawing-boards and computers, conjuring up the magical dramas of *Pocahontas* and *The Lion King*, sending Donald Duck and Goofy on yet more new adventures, and keeping alive the fame of the Walt Disney Company, which all began with Mickey Mouse and his companions. What should it look like? For the architect Robert A.M. Stern there was only one answer: the cartoon company's new headquarters should look as if it came from a cartoon world itself. In his words, "I grew up with cartoons, which always took place in some fantastic city of the future. I finally got to build that vision."

The new complex on the edge of the Disney studio site in Burbank is signposted by a gigantic cone, a huge replica of Mickey Mouse's magic hat from *Fantasia*. At the centre is a trio of studio buildings which look as if Peter Behrens' legendary AEG turbine-hall had been beamed to Ducksburg. The long front of the building can be seen from the Ventura Freeway; its entrance section presents a stylized reference to American "streamline" designs, with an atrium lobby under its semi-glazed tip. Stern creates a pastiche of modern architectural trends, playing freely with styles, materials and colours on the exterior and the interior. However, he makes sparing use of direct references to Disney's comic world. For all its showiness, the building is organized in a thoroughly modern way. The drawing studios are spacious, flexibly arranged loft spaces. Cables, service pipes and structural elements run visibly across the barrel ceilings of the top floor. What looks like a starry sky is in fact a black felt-covered ceiling dotted with steel rivets.

In addition to Stern, Michael Eisner, Chairman and CEO, has commissioned some other world-famous architects like Frank O. Gehry, Aldo Rossi, Arata Isozaki and Michael Graves. Stern himself designed a series of nostalgic tourist buildings for this client before he was finally able to make his own mark with the Feature Animation Building, "a jolly collision of spaces and symbols dedicated to the serious work of being silly" (*New York Times*).

Opposite top:
The bold use of colour and form lends an air of fantasy to Stern's design of the entrance façade. Access is gained via the Mickey Mouse Sorcerer's hat tower. To the left, three vaulted studio wings house the creative workforce.

Opposite left:
The building's primary circulation and communal spaces are contained in the sweeping streamlined structure. The corrugated metal south façade rises at an angle to the maximum permitted height limit of the site. The lower portion in stucco is partially glazed.

Opposite right:
Lit from above by a skylight, the office of the head of the animation division, Roy Disney, is located within the tip of the cone. Mickey's hat motif is continued in the shelving unit.

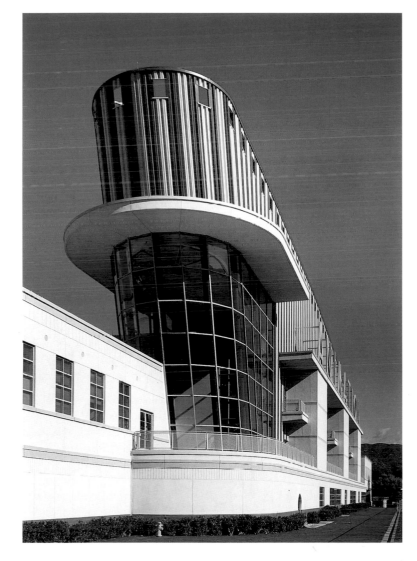

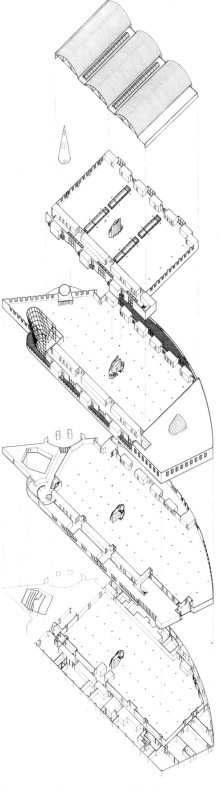

Cables, service pipes and structural elements are an integral part of the design, running visibly across the barrel vault of the top floor. What looks at first like a star-studded sky is in reality metal rivets in a cloth-covered ceiling.

The exploded axonometric of the four-storey building illustrates the complexity of organization involved in housing over 700 employees. The structure includes archives and computers on the lower level, post production on the ground floor, animation on the second floor, and story development on the third, the whole unified by a centrally placed grand staircase.

Reception is located under the tilted form
of the glazed atrium. The terrazzo floor
shows a film-spool motif.

CLM/BBDO,
PARIS, FRANCE

ARCHITECT/INTERIOR DESIGNER:
JEAN NOUVEL ET ASSOCIÉS
1994

For Jean Nouvel, the master of thrilling architectural abstractions, this is a project of striking metaphorical simplicity. The headquarters of the Paris advertising agency CLM/BBDO sits like a stranded, rusting ship in a waterlogged setting not far from the banks of the Seine. Barges and floating homes are moored on the quayside of Issy-les-Moulineaux on the Île-Saint-Germain: this area of the Paris suburbs is definitely not one of the capital's more upmarket addresses. The company's chief executive Philippe Michel chose the site with care, and commissioned Nouvel to create a landmark in this colourful no-man's land: the Arche Nova is intended as an unmistakable, image-defining piece of corporate architecture which will act as a creative driving force for the company's development.

The four-storey building changes its appearance with the weather. When it is warm and sunny, the huge glass wings of the roof open automatically; they close as if by magic when the weather changes. Here, with his usual consum-mate skill, Nouvel rehearses his favourite themes of containment and transparency. From the outside, the solid closed mass of the building is relieved only at night by the light of the windows; the inside, by contrast, reveals an airy, open style of construction surrounded by galleries. An escalator leads into the building at the stern of the agency "ship"; the silver-grey of the foyer and the adjoining extended atrium courtyard is intended to be reminiscent of the "mother-of-pearl sheen of an oyster" (Nouvel).

Transparency and borderlessness are core elements of the internal design, evident in the railings running along the internal walkways (which merge into benches and writing desks), in the translucent sliding partitions and glass-slatted doors of the offices, and in the impressive mechanical blinds of the large conference rooms which jut out into the narrow ends of the ship's light interior. The space is divided up flexibly, following the different functions of the agency's departments. The ground and first floors (below the level of the main entrance) house the service departments; the larger creative workshops are on the second floor, the sales departments on the top floor; the company directors are at the front, in the bow of the ship. As well as designing the interior, Nouvel also created much of the building's furniture.

Above:
The "Arche Nouvel" at night near the river moorings on the Seine. Lighted windows provide the only signs of life in an otherwise rusty-looking hull, designed deliberately to mimic the ravages of time. The roof automatically opens and closes in response to weather conditions.

Opposite:
The spacious interiors are arranged on three gallery floors surrounding two open spaces. Nouvel's metaphor of an oyster's rough and dark shell containing a hidden pearl is demonstrated in his translucent and smooth design, which uses glass, metal, aluminium and a holographic material that refracts sunlight. The furniture was designed for the most part by Nouvel.

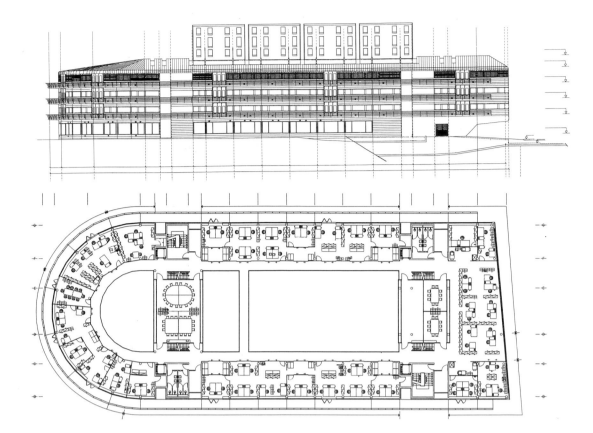

Left:

Elevation, plans of the first and second floors, and section. The offices open on to the galleries and are arranged around the atrium.

Opposite:

What looks like a sports hall is the core of the CLM/BBDO headquarters. The empty space serves as an exhibition and event area and is also made available for staff sports activities.

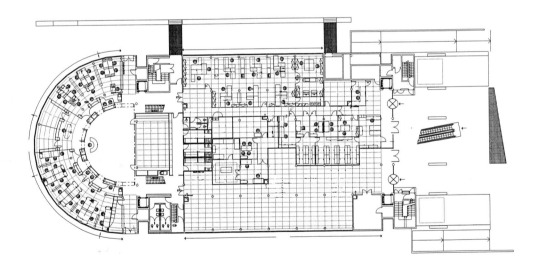

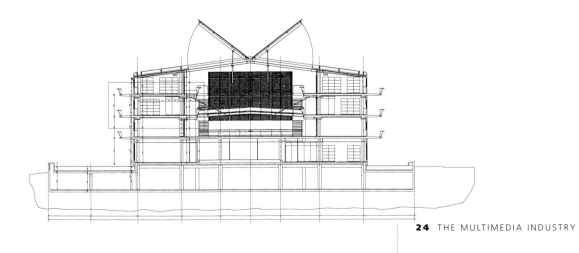

PIXELPARK,
BERLIN, GERMANY

INTERIOR DESIGNER:
WOLFRAM POPP
1994

While most people were just talking about multimedia, a few young self-starters were taking their first steps in the multimedia business, which soon became very lucrative. One of these self-made entrepreneurs is Paulus Neef of Berlin, whose company Pixelpark has developed rapidly into one of Europe's most successful producers of interactive information and entertainment products. Growth brought a new shareholder – the Bertelsmann group, one of the world's largest media companies – as well as the need for larger premises. For its new headquarters Pixelpark chose one storey of a Berlin factory building, with an area of over 800 square metres. The interior design was to match the company's innovative outlook: it needed a creative work-shop for the professional designers of virtual experience products, with team workspaces for three to ten people, and areas for meetings and events.

Architect Wolfram Popp started from the observation that efficiency in this particular production site was not to be achieved or contained by the linear, rational structures of other companies, and he designed a flexible office environ-ment structured by its movable fittings. "Here success is measured not by productivity, but by imaginative ways of using ideas". The design makes dynamic use of the relation-ship between closed and open areas: the dividing elements are transparent and flexible, and the office space as a whole is in a constant state of flux. The area for conferences and presentations can be organized as an "aquarium with a surf board" (Popp) according to requirements: all the movable walls can also be converted into projection areas using com-puter-controlled touchscreen panels; the desk system con-sists of six individual units which can be used separately. The working areas are arranged in "blobs": rounded, partly open and movable constructions of glass and plywood. The choice of materials and the overall effect are minimalist in style. Without resorting to futuristic special effects, Popp has succeeded in creating an office world of the future. This suc-cess may have its roots in the architect's past: the self-taught Popp started out as a set-designer for science-fiction films.

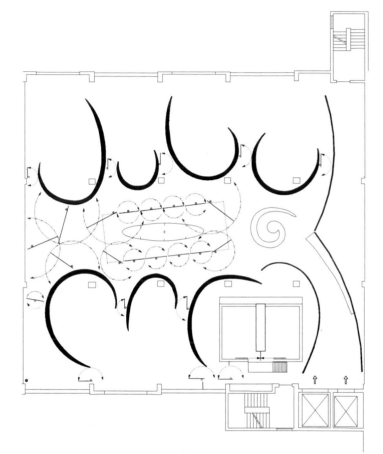

The floor plan (*above*) shows the flowing dynamic layout of the former factory floor. The finished scheme (*opposite*) consists of self-contained movable semicircular workstations surrounding a communal meeting area. Each module is constructed from glass and plywood.

The conference area or presentation room
is formed from movable semi-opaque
walls which at the touch of a computer-
controlled screen are transformed into
projection areas.

INTERIOR DESIGNER:
GAETANO PESCE
1994–96

Eccentric office environments designed by artist-architects seem to have become a core ingredient of corporate identity. However, Jay Chiat, head of the American advertising agency Chiat/Day, is concerned with more than creating an image: the company's offices are intended as avant-garde models of a virtualized working world focused on computer-based team work.

The most radical architectural demonstration of Chiat's ideas is located not far from Wall Street, in a skyscraper on the southern tip of Manhattan, overlooking the Statue of Liberty. Here the Italian avant-garde designer Gaetano Pesce, who works in New York, has created a surreal cybervillage for Net surfers, on an area of 2,700 square metres. This is no ordinary office: employees do not come in and sit down at desks; they enter a brightly coloured playground, an anarchic world made of amorphous shapes, garish colours and unexpected juxtapositions. They get their note-

book and files from a "kissing-lips kiosk" in the morning, and plug into a felt-wrapped trolley to invent new advertising ideas on-line. "The only way you can change the way people work is by changing the environment in which they work. All our lives we know where we're going to sit. Now we're saying what you need to know is what you're going to do when you come in. And that's a big traumatic behavioral change" (Jay Chiat).

In fact the real office revolution here takes place not in Pesce's eccentric setting but on the computer screens. The communications software "Oxygen", developed specially for Chiat/Day, provides and creates the organizational structure which supports all the agency's work. It connects the New York branch with other branches; it is a design tool, a storage system and a medium for information and telecommunications all rolled into one. Here the functions and performance of digital networking take clear precedence over the spatial configuration of the office world. With this loss of significance, the office becomes an arbitrary environment, a space for experiments. In 1996, Pesce was able to add another storey to his bizarre office fantasy when Chiat/Day merged with its former competitor TBWA.

Above:
Hand-painted sketches illustrate ideas for entrances to individual project rooms.

Opposite:
Gaetano Pesce's drawing of the floor plan (*below*) reveals an architectural painting as the origin of the design (*above*).

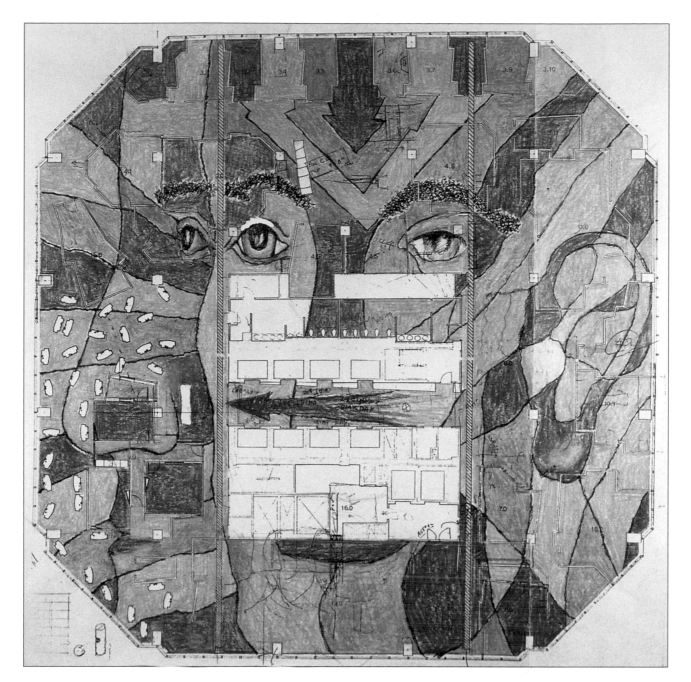

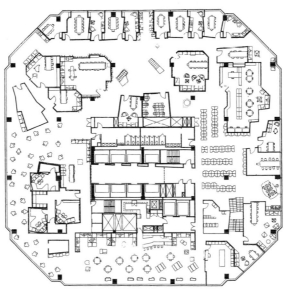

Reminiscent more of a social meeting-point than an office, Pesce's solution has avoided any signs of a functional working space. Employees conduct their business in front of laptops in a garish café setting. The floor is painted in quick-setting resin, thus suggesting the need for a spontaneous act of creation. The chairs are in cast resin designed by Pesce.

Below:
Computer workstations are located in brightly coloured felt-covered trolleys on wheels. The walls to the rear are made from discarded videos and mobile phones set in resin.

Project Room No. 1, and Pesce's sketch for the bottle-shaped doorway.

Opposite top:
Movable stairways are used for room division or as seating. In the background can be seen the wall of light with fully adjustable light sources and cutaway openings to alternative work spaces beyond.

Opposite bottom:
Typical office area showing unusual juxtapositions, surreal use of motif, and doodles by Pesce in the quick-setting resin.

INTERIOR DESIGNER:
ANDERSON/SCHWARTZ ARCHITECTS
1995

Muted lights, angled walls, forked corridors, bare concrete, a blue shimmer of light through open doors: visitors arriving on the tenth floor of this ordinary commercial block in New York's SoHo might be forgiven for thinking they have wandered on to an Expressionist film set. In fact, the former printshop is the home of SMA Video, a young company active in the increasingly lucrative sector encompassing film and digital production technologies. It is a fair-sized operation, with 20 employees and an office space measuring 2,150 square metres.

SMA Video's offices are a living illustration of the changes taking place in the media world. The old tangible realities of word and image have disappeared into the virtual world of computers: the clatter of printing presses has been replaced by the whirr of high-performance computers and editing units. The office environment for this new working world fulfils two functions. For the experts at their computer screens, it serves to facilitate concentration and communication. For the company's clients, from the worlds of advertising, film and television, it provides a visual correlative for the secrets hidden away in the ordinary-looking machines.

The architects Anderson/Schwartz designed the area as a twilight zone. In fact, they covered hardly any of the existing windows, using dividing units and partition walls to create a dimmed lighting effect which enhances the impact of the interior design, as well as sparing the screen-fixed eyes of the company's employees. The building's original pillars were left standing and the main thoroughfare, called the Canyon, curves around the dark columns with its angled walls. Problems of cabling and temperature regulation are inevitable in high-tech offices: here they are solved in a pragmatic and effective way. SMA devised its own colour-coding system for the cable network, making sense of the mass of computer cables running through floors, ceilings and cable ducts hanging from the walls.

Opposite top:
The reception area is a haven of light at the end of the "Canyon". Elsewhere the lighting is kept deliberately subdued so as not to dazzle employees coming directly from the studios.

Opposite bottom:
A digital editing room with state-of-the-art technical equipment is finished in assorted materials including cherry, maple, limestone and pietra cardoza. The editing rooms are accessed from a perimeter "street" which acts as a buffer from the light, noise and vibration.

Below:
Floor plan. The offices are designed around a "canyon" and "bunker" design, with sound stage and shops behind the south wall of the "canyon", and machine room and mechanical equipment beyond the north. The offices and art department curve around existing concrete columns. All volumes are pulled back from the windows giving a sense of displacement to anyone entering the building.

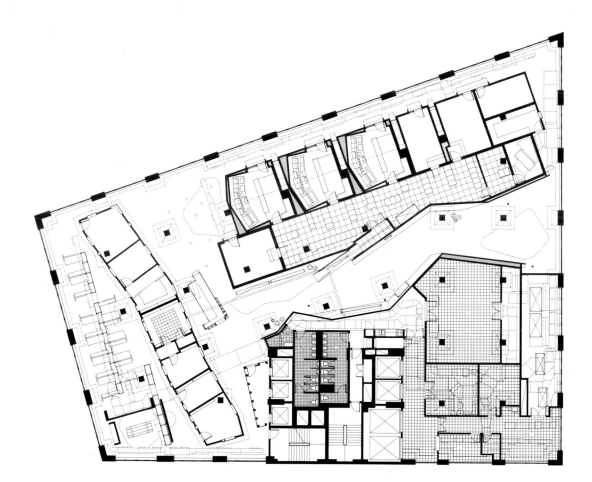

Opposite top:
View from reception: the cable work necessary to maintain a high-tech studio runs through floors and hangs from the ceiling in specially designed cable ducts.

Opposite bottom:
The "Canyon" (the corridor leading off the reception area) is clad with MDF panels on a sliding modular grid which allows cubic Lexan window boxes to extrude through the wall.

THOMSON MULTIMEDIA, INDIANAPOLIS, USA

ARCHITECT:
HALDEMAN, POWELL, JOHNS ARCHITECTS
ARCHITECT/INTERIOR DESIGNER:
MICHAEL GRAVES
1994

The US subsidiary of the French electronics group Thomson commissioned its new head office in 1994. The building, with a floor space of 19,500 square metres, is a classic example of conventional office architecture overlaid with cosmetic surgery. Thomson has suffered more than most from the ongoing crises in the consumer electronics sector: it is not surprising that the company should look to enhance its image in this way. As electronics hardware loses its appeal

of prefabricated concrete panels. By contrast, he turned what had been a mundane entrance area into an architectural focal point, adding a yellow portal with a superstructure of double pillars to the terracotta-coloured cube. On the interior is a blue atrium surrounded with pillars, soaring up to a shallow glass dome.

As for most of his projects, Graves also designed the interiors of the public areas. These include the viewing gallery in the top storey, where clients and business partners

(its products are bland and interchangeable), it is seeking to compensate by borrowing from the more colourful, glamorous world of software products.

Neo-classical architect Michael Graves, creator of numerous Disney projects, was commissioned to design alterations to the project after construction work had started. His interventions focused on the façade and the central entrance area of the four-storey, elongated building. On the façade Graves restricted himself to adding a grey-green chessboard pattern

are shown the latest models of Thomson brands RCA, GE and ProScan. The architect described the central motif of his successful alterations as "a distinctive sense of joy". Whether business has improved since Thomson Multimedia has moved into its new head office is not disclosed. However, the company can at least be pleased with the success and speed of its architectural rescue operation. Graves's substantial modifications delayed the building's completion by no more than two months.

Opposite:

Michael Graves revamped this ordinary office scheme, with an abstract classical portico in bright colours and a chequered concrete façade.

Right:

The viewing gallery on the top floor was designed as a showcase to exhibit the latest product ranges, and serves as a customer information area.

Below:

The Directors' board room.

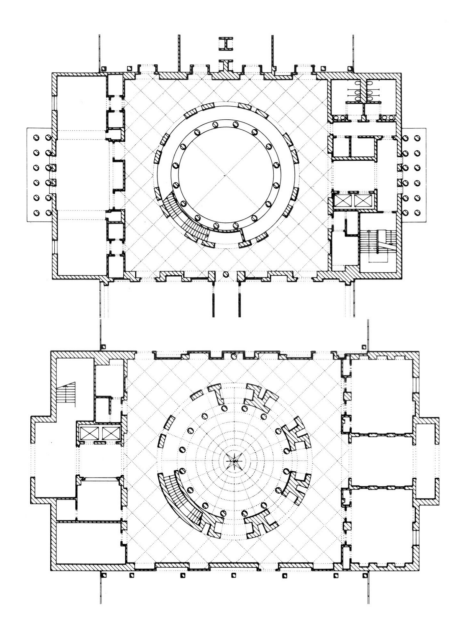

Left:

The floor plan and section, showing Graves's design intervention. The building is organized as two office wings on either side of a top-lit cubic pavilion containing a cylindrical atrium and grand staircase.

Opposite:

The atrium is described by Graves as "a building within a building" and is the focal point of the design. It rises through the four storeys and is surrounded by a ceremonial staircase and blue stucco columns.

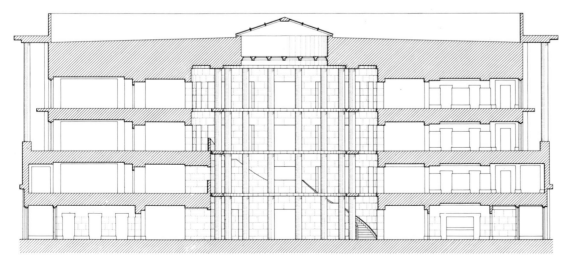

TELECOM CENTER,
TOKYO, JAPAN

ARCHITECT:
HELLMUTH, OBATA +
KASSABAUM/NISSOKEN ARCHITECTS
1996

The huge Teleport Town project in Tokyo opens up new territory in a thoroughly literal sense: it is being built on land reclaimed from the sea. Nearly 70,000 people will work here, creating wealth through satellite-based communications systems, computer networks and interactive technology. Teleport's nerve centre and showpiece is the Telecom Center, which cost $321 million (£207 million) to build: it is a dazzling creation consisting of two 24-storey office blocks, joined at ground level by a five-storey atrium and at the top by a huge bridge construction. Structurally the building is composed of squares and cube shapes, varied by some circular and cylindrical elements. American architects Hellmuth, Obata and Kassabaum designed the main body of the building, its outer layer and public areas: they "viewed the architectural image and technological requirements of the building to be an exciting and significant challenge".

The building's abstract external appearance, with its blue mirror façade made of aluminium and glass, is intended as a metaphor of the Information Age. Telecom Center is the headquarters of the Teleport Company, founded by public and private investors to manage and develop the new commercial district. Fibreglass Local Area Networks are controlled from here, and there are television studios and the CATV transmission centre for digital, interactive multi-channel television. The impressive bridge construction is not just a show piece: it is also a functional operating platform for a dozen large satellite dishes and other aerials which could not have been accommodated in any other way. The whole complex is a "smart building" with a fully integrated electronic facility management system regulating energy supply, security systems and computer networks. To the east it is connected to a lower structure which supplies the heating and air-conditioning systems for the whole of Teleport Town.

Telecom Center has a floor space of 157,000 square metres in all: half of this is let to other companies, the remainder houses the administrative offices of the operating company, various telecommunications and television

facilities, video conference rooms, shops and gastronomy (including a panoramic restaurant with observatory in the bridge section). In contrast to the building's electronic sophistication, its offices are designed in a disconcertingly traditional style. Yet this is perhaps not so surprising: for all the futuristic wizardry, human needs remain the same.

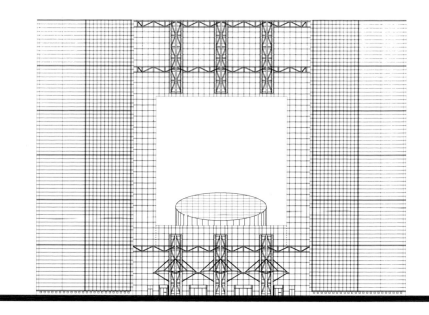

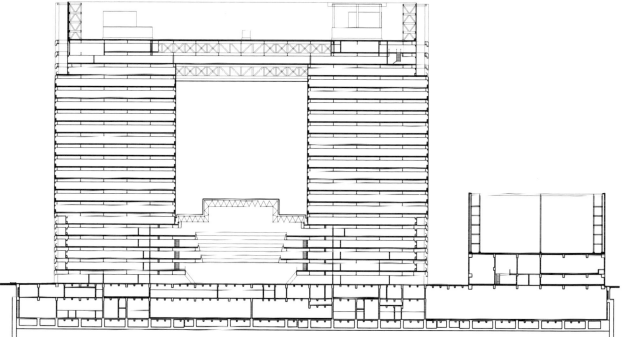

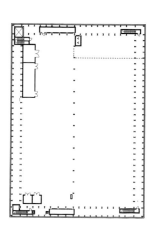

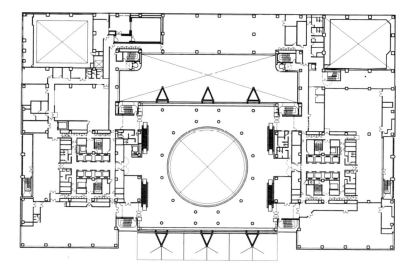

Opposite:
The two office towers of the Telecom Center are linked by the bridging satellite platform which contains more than a dozen huge antennae dishes.

Left:
Elevation, with neighbouring power-station for the whole Telecom district.

Below:
Section and ground-floor plan.

Right:
The cylindrical atrium contrasts with the cubic principle of the building design.

Below:
Public spaces, such as the reception lobby, provide an interlude of glass, steel and stone.

VG-HUSET, OSLO, NORWAY

ARCHITECT:
LUND & SLATTO ARKITEKTER
1994

This building is set in the historic heart of Oslo, with government ministries, churches and grand hotels among its eminent neighbours. This provides a rather intimidating setting for the upstart newcomer made of steel and glass. Especially as its pedigree is hardly upper-class: VG stands for *Verdens Gang*, the most successful and aggressive of Norway's tabloid newspapers. Admittedly the tabloid sensationalists share the new newspaper building with their more serious colleagues from the *Afterposten*, as well as the headquarters of publishing company Schibsted (which has several television companies and various activities in the new media). Nonetheless, the building is named after VG, its most notorious inhabitant.

The architecture has added undisputed quality to the venture. Lund & Slatto's design sets international standards in stylistic and technical terms, perfectly suiting its context and function. The building has ten storeys and 32,000 square metres of usable floor space. Its external transparency is no empty gesture: the ground floor of the soaring atrium is a public passageway with shops, a restaurant and a supermarket. The offices are arranged around this central courtyard, organized mainly in complementary groups: small individual workrooms are set around meeting rooms and communal areas. The client wanted the project to have state-of-the-art communications and building technologies, with fully computerized 24-hour facility management. All room features are centrally regulated, and the security system encompasses all public and non-public areas. The IT system includes networks for data transfer, telecommunications, video and television transmissions, and satellite connections. However, these high-tech functions and features are never obtrusive.

The architects' sensitive use of materials and their sure sense for impressive, but not overwhelming, proportions combine to create a unique and satisfying modernist design. The building can even allow itself the luxury of a casual note here and there, with wicker seats and bistro furniture in the glazed roof gallery and elsewhere.

Left:
Well-tempered intruder: Oslo's most modern publishing house.

Opposite:
The transparency of the glass and aluminium structure is in direct contrast to the rough, grey granite of Henrik Bull's Finance Ministry (1904) which is located directly opposite.

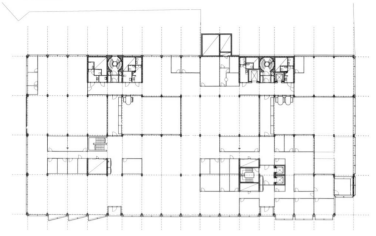

Left and opposite (top):
The offices are arranged in galleries around an impressive glazed-roof atrium which also contains shops, a restaurant and a supermarket.

Opposite (bottom):
As a result of the use of glazed partitions, the working areas, although individually enclosed, have an open atmosphere.

Below:
First- and fourth-floor plans, and section.

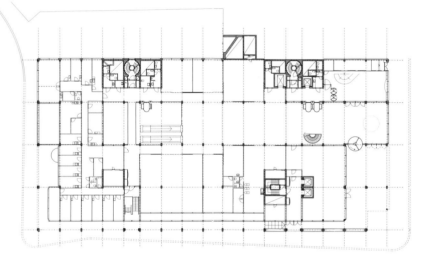

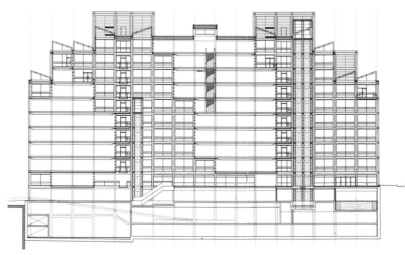

LEO BURNETT, LONDON, UK

ARCHITECT:
YRM/STANTON-WILLIAMS
INTERIOR DESIGNER:
FLETCHER PRIEST
1994

The typical terracotta façade reveals this building's origins: it is one of a group put up in south and west London in the early years of this century, by Harrods department store. What is now the London office of American advertising agency Leo Burnett once used to house stockrooms, workshops and garages. At the time of its construction, in the middle of World War I, the building was not completed according to plan. Later brick-built additions disfigured the original structure, prompting the architects to take a radical approach when it was converted into an office complex: apart from the original façade scarcely a single stone remained in place.

The ambitious project was well worth its £15-million price tag, as the developer's company took the bold step of commissioning architects Alan Stanton and Paul Williams, famous for their arts projects. Their design complements and encases the historical building with a clearly articulated construction which follows the proportions of the original plans, and consists of a concrete supporting structure with a glass curtain façade. On the outside the concrete sections are partially covered with natural stone, emphasizing the interplay of past and present. This dialogue is echoed in the atrium, where four storeys of granite slabs with cut-in window-openings contrast with the transparent glass galleries. The building has 8,300 square metres of office space in the upper four storeys, with 3,900 square metres of shop space, a restaurant, a warehouse, and a car park on the ground floor and in the basement.

The interior designers Fletcher Priest were commissioned to design the offices: their task was to develop flexible, team-orientated spaces which would be suitable for all forms of multimedia communication. "Advertising agencies are at the forefront of changes in the patterns and nature of office-based work", says Keith Priest, referring to the building's highly sophisticated electronic systems, which include the latest interactive building and lighting technology. However, all these high-tech refinements are carefully concealed, and the overall impression is of an elegant and sober modernism: without doubt one of the chief merits of this grand scheme.

Opposite top:
The building, designed by Stevens and Munt as warehousing and workshop facilities for Harrods, is topped by a stepped-back extension in red sandstone and glass, with a glass and metal curtain wall. It has been designed to reflect the rhythm of structure, scale and proportion of the existing building.

Opposite bottom:
A simple yet adaptable floor plan was developed, creating individual, acoustically separated working spaces, and large communal areas set around a central atrium.

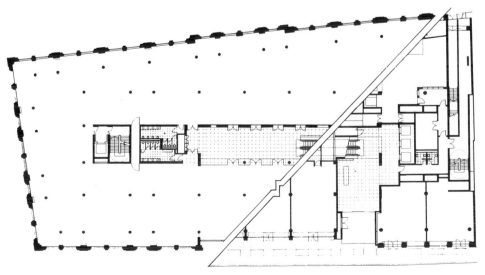

Left:
Working area, showing a metal-clad circular tea point which doubles as a poster drum and focal meeting place. Workstations can be varied and are based on minimum use of components.

Below:
The masonry-clad reception area at one end of the atrium is reached by escalators rising from the ground-floor lobby.

Opposite:
The light well is 30 metres long: to the north is a solid stone wall and to the south a transparent glass partition, a successful symbiosis of old and new carried through from the façade.

2

ADVANCED OFFICE ENVIRONMENTS

The international finance system is pointing the way forward. In the post-bureaucratic world of the on-line office, administrative processes are being taken over by electronic systems whose constant streams of data transcend time-boundaries, making the question of location irrelevant. Through all sectors of industry, office functions are changing. Hierarchies are being dismantled, company headquarters are shrinking, workforce reductions are set to reach unprecedented levels. Rationalization, project-based work and outsourcing are the keywords for the future. Companies will be fragmented into small team units (often using temporary, freelance workers) which communicate with other units using e-mail, databases, host systems, intranets, workflow systems and electronic conferencing. The rapid devaluation of traditional administrative structures has made those offices that do survive all the more important in terms of style. Architectural display effects can take central stage: and they are no longer reserved exclusively for client-orientated public and semi-public areas: in this office revolution, the remaining employees are also treated to technological, ergonomic and ecological refinements.

ING BANK, BUDAPEST, HUNGARY

ARCHITECT/INTERIOR DESIGNER:
EEA ERICK VAN EGERAAT ASSOCIATED ARCHITECTS
1995

In the early 1990s, the capitals of Eastern Europe became strategic locations for many leading western companies as they sought to establish a presence in these new markets. Large numbers of financial companies have acquired or built offices in Budapest and Prague; Nationale Nederlanden, a subsidiary of the ING Bank group, stands out among them for the high quality of its buildings. The Dutch company has sought to export the best of Western architecture into these cities, which were cut off from contemporary trends for many years. The deconstructionist Frank O. Gehry designed an angular office building in Prague; he is soon to be followed by French hypermodernist Jean Nouvel.

The Dutch architect Erick van Egeraat, a leading figure of the "new sobriety", was commissioned to design the Budapest branch of the ING Bank. Egeraat was formerly a member of the Mecanoo group of architects, where he established his reputation with a series of uncompromising new buildings. In this instance, however, he was asked to restore and convert a protected neo-classical nineteenth-century building right at the heart of the city. This was uncharted territory for the architect, and he found his bearings by making the central ambivalence of his task into the focal point of his design. "Through restoration the building has now become far more pure than the original. But I really very much wanted to add something completely new to the old atmosphere. I wanted to add a pure space on the roof" (Van Egeraat).

The architect converted what had been an open courtyard into an atrium: above it, in place of the conventional glass dome, is an amorphous shape which appears to be suspended in mid-air. This large roof construction (the "whale") is made of wood, aluminium and glass, and encroaches upon the new office area below; it contains a conference hall. Egeraat's design, which included the building's furnishings, manages to be both respectful and uncompromising.

The transformation of the nineteenth-century landmark building starts at the top, where architect Van Egeraat landed a big "whale".

Left:

Inside the belly of the "whale" is the ING Bank "boardroom". Exposed laminated wooden ribs and lift mechanism make up a spartan interior.

Opposite:

The ash wood and glass construction sits on a glazed roof which is constructed from glass panes, supported on glass beams without the use of a metal frame. The beams rest on stainless-steel adjustable "forks".

Left:

The whale-like construction presses down through the fabric of the main building and penetrates through the top two office floors of the building which were added by the architect.

Opposite top:

Front and side elevations. The "Italianate" main fabric of the building has been restored to its nineteenth-century splendour, maintaining the internal spatial divisions of existing rooms. The original open courtyard, however, has been turned into an atrium, covered not by a conventional skylight but by the amorphous addition.

Opposite bottom:

Top floor and roof plans illustrate how the "whale" has been hidden away from the street below.

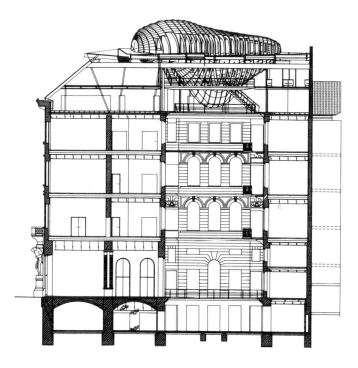

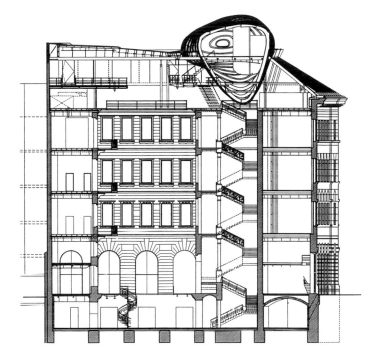

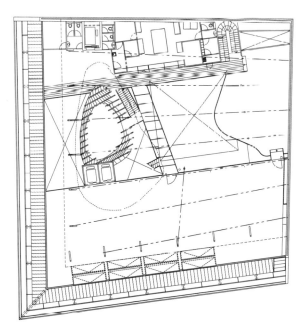

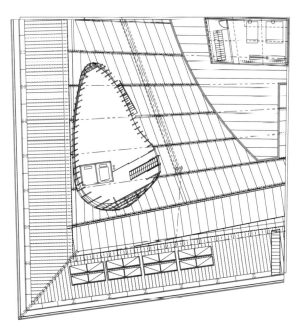

BANCO SANTANDER, MADRID, SPAIN

ARCHITECT/INTERIOR DESIGNER:
HANS HOLLEIN
1993

The new headquarters of Banco Santander, one of Spain's leading financial institutions, is set within a group of protected buildings on the Castellana, one of the grand boulevards of Madrid. It has 23,000 square metres of floor space on a plot measuring 2,200 square metres. The planning authorities stipulated that the original façades should be retained and restored, which meant that architectural intervention was restricted to the interior and the courtyard area. This still gave architect Hans Hollein ample scope for creating one of his dramatic projects. Hollein had used the rotunda motif in other buildings: here he elevated it to monumental status. His domed cylinder is 27 metres high and 23 metres in diameter; it is slightly wider at the top than the bottom. With its staircases, galleries, glazed façades and bright surfaces the light hall is a public space which draws visitors towards it as soon as they are inside the bank: "The building does not reveal itself until you are beyond the entrance" (Hollein).

The rotunda is set at an angle to the original building (whose residential apartments were converted into offices),

thus placing the old structure in a new context. Hollein's construction (which he irreverently called a "distributor construction") respects the old floor-plan by transposing it and throwing it into relief. The impressive spatial effects tend to obscure the fact that this is the nerve centre of the bank's computer operations. But this is probably intentional. Just as a striking piece of contemporary architecture is hidden behind the historical façade, so the banking business with its global electronic networks retires behind Hollein's artistic creation. In any case the ordinary offices are not open to the public and their functional interiors were not included in the eminent architect's brief.

Below:
Section through the court and front of the building. The shallow-domed rotunda is set at an angle. Existing rooms, protected as historic apartment buildings, have been converted from residential spaces to offices.

Opposite:
Looking down into the main focal point of the building: a central rotunda which is 27 metres high and 23 metres in diameter.

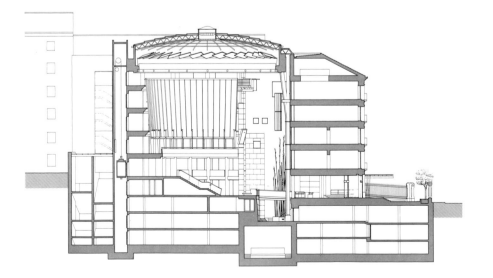

63**63** ADVANCED OFFICE ENVIRONMENTS

Below:
The aerial perspective highlights the fact that the rotunda is wider at the top than at the bottom.

Right:
Detail of the ground floor rotunda with stairs to the passage leading through to the historic part of the building.

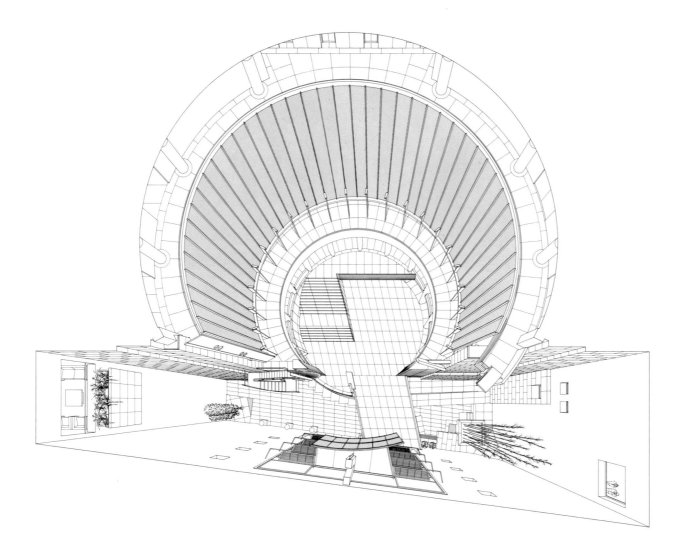

BANQUE DE LUXEMBOURG, LUXEMBOURG

ARCHITECT:
ARQUITECTONICA
INTERIOR DESIGNER:
JEAN-MICHEL WILMOTTE
1994

In recent years Luxembourg has become established as a major international finance centre and a haven for private assets. The rise of Luxembourg's banking sector has spawned a high-profile building boom: the fast-growing financial institutions can afford to employ internationally renowned architects. Most of these showpiece projects have been built on the outskirts of the capital. However, this was not the case with the new headquarters of the long-established Banque de Luxembourg: the bank commissioned the American team of architects Arquitectonica to create its first European building in the heart of the city, on Boulevard Royal.

Arquitectonica, based in Miami, was used to producing buildings on a very different scale: in Luxembourg it had to be content with a plot of just 3,400 square metres. The architects had to provide the required floor space of over 21,000 square metres without exceeding statutory limits on building height or eliminating all open spaces. To do this they dug deep into the Luxembourg rock: the six-storey building which stands on the corner plot today, a smart collage of two cubes and a neat stub-tower, is only the tip of this financial iceberg. There are eight storeys below ground level, reaching to a depth of 28 metres. "In the present situation of growing competition, architecture plays a very specific role for our company. It is above all a marketing instrument,

a way of presenting our image", says Robert Reckinger, chairman of the bank's board of directors. Together with Arquitectonica the bank developed a concept which turned the restrictions of the site into a metaphor for financial business, with its traditional values of security, trust and discretion, presented in a thoroughly contemporary style.

Visitors who enter the building from the Boulevard are led down into the basement which houses the large banking-hall and most of the consultation rooms, receiving ample daylight from the glass tower building. However, most customers arrive by car, park in one of the lavishly-appointed car parks and take a lift to the banking area. The bank's business is mainly concerned with giving investment advice and managing stock-exchange transactions, so there are no hordes of customers to disturb the formal, dignified atmosphere. Jean-Michel Wilmotte, the interior designer, based in Paris, proved to be an ideal partner for Arquitectonica. The spartan elegance of the building's interior design accentuates the quality of the materials used, perfectly matching the stylish architectural import from Florida. The new bank headquarters is fully equipped to play its part in today's highly computerized financial world. Not only the dealing rooms but all consultation rooms have on-line access to global stock-exchange data; the cable network is 90 kilometres in length.

Opposite:

A coloured representational CAD-drawing shows the main volumes of the bank. The perforated stone section cantilevers to align with the street, whilst the glass wing acts as a focal reference. The third volume is clad in black granite and serves as a spoil to the other parts of the building.

Below:

The transparency of the elliptical tower is in direct contrast with the solidity of the block it straddles. Used for special functions, it also houses a boardroom, library reading rooms, a conference room and lobby atrium. The stone block is studded with a regular pattern of square amber-glassed windows designed to blend with the tonality of vernacular building materials.

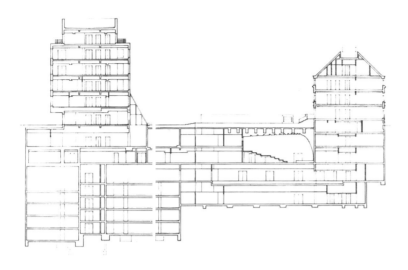

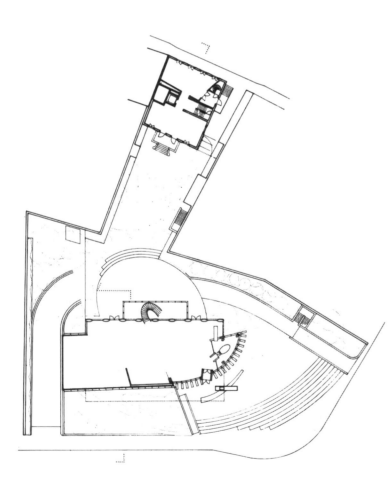

Top left:

Elevation: two-thirds of the complex was constructed below street level in order to comply with height restrictions. This accommodates the main banking floor, trading rooms, computer centre, vaults and a community auditorium. The building on the right is a restored historic villa used today for functions and receptions.

Bottom left:

Ground-floor plan of the glass tower, showing the conference room above and the atrium below. The historic guest villa is situated at the top.

Opposite:

The interior of the atrium is stone-clad and is overlooked by balconies from the floors above and also by an oval-shaped open lift.

Below:

The boardroom follows the wedge-shape form of the tower in which it is situated. The pattern of the windows is echoed in a recessed lighting fixture above the main conference table.

ISAR BÜRO PARK, MUNICH, GERMANY

ARCHITECT:
MAKI AND ASSOCIATES
1995

The construction of the new Munich airport at Erdinger Moos, well outside the city, promised to bring prosperity to this rural area. Thankfully for the landscape and environment, many of the speculative projects have not come to fruition. Among the large commercial projects that have been completed is Fumihiko Maki's Isar Büro Park, a textbook example of how a building can be integrated thoughtfully with its natural setting, and one which should be held up as a model for future developments in the area.

The Japanese architect won an international competition for the project. His design divides the generous brief for

over 68,300 square metres of usable floor space across two office buildings and nine smaller units. The complex as a whole is kept at a low level, four or five storeys high, and its proportions reflect those of the surrounding landscape. "The project concept arose from our desire to create a new type of working environment for high-technology industries while preserving and using to the fullest advantage an existing rural landscape" (Maki). The transition between interior

and exterior, between the building and the natural environment, is accentuated through the use of bridging elements such as the glass screens that run across the roof surfaces, set at an angle. Open, glass-covered paths lead through gardens from one building to another.

Maki's first European building also stands out for the type of detail (in terms of both design and execution) that is unusual in commercial projects of this type. Terraces and atria are used to vary the spatial effects, as well as bringing more daylight into the building. An ingenious system of aluminium blinds and cold-water pipes in the ceilings protects the building from excessive sunlight and heat. Maki's client, a property subsidiary of Germany's largest bank, wanted this showpiece project to be an "office park for the twenty-first century" at the same time as enhancing its own image. Thanks to Maki, this seems to have been a complete success.

Left:
Ambitious office development near Munich airport.

Opposite top:
Site plan showing how Maki has divided the office-park complex between two large office buildings and nine smaller units connected by open-air walkways.

Opposite:
Ground- and second-floor plans of office block no. 1 (*left*) and ground- and first-floor plans of office block no. 5 (*right*). Both structures are developed around multi-storey atriums. The spatial divisions are cleanly organized on the standard "belt-plan" of enclosed single rooms, but have been opened out to create gaps for courts and terraces which act as communal areas and allow light to flood in from the glazed roofs.

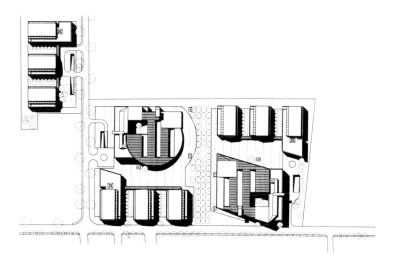

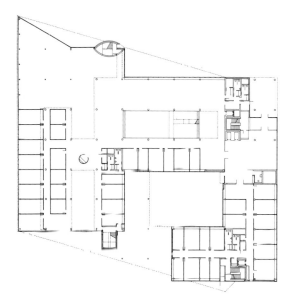

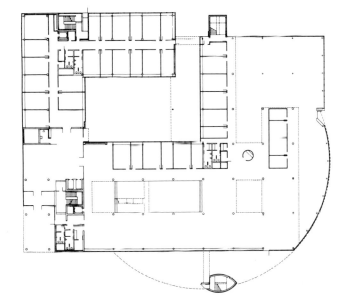

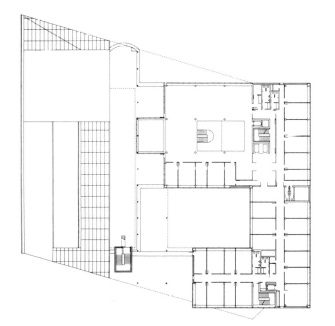

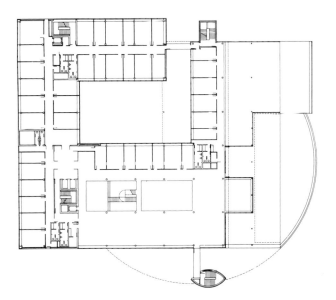

Above left:

The staircases are an important feature of the overall interior design. Free-standing, with wooden steps and handrails and perforated metal landings, they act as sculptural elements.

Above right:

Office spaces are located below aluminium blinds with cold-water pipes, which act as a protection from excessive sunlight and heat. The interiors are fitted in a mixture of aluminium, natural materials and polished stucco.

Opposite:

Façades of office blocks nos. 1 and 5. Glass and aluminium with slender profiles have been used for the main surfaces, articulated by the use of granite cladding. The glass roof is designed to continually reflect and filter the changing sky. Maki has used basic geometric shapes, superimposing circles, rectangles and triangles.

NTT, TOKYO, JAPAN

ARCHITECT:
CESAR PELLI & ASSOCIATES
1995

The Nippon Telegraph and Telephone Corporation, NTT for short, is one of the largest telecommunications groups in the world. As we embark on the new information age, with its data super-highways and audiovisual networking, the company headquarters of a global player like this has to be an arena for the latest digital technologies: "a living showcase of NTT services and products for the multimedia business environment", in the company's own words. Here every workspace is an interactive nexus of complex EDI and communications systems, giving access to information and on-line services in word, image and sound. The building management systems (including power supply and security) are fully computerized.

What is more, in New York architect Cesar Pelli the company engaged an accomplished stylist who produced a text-book skyscraper to fit the tiny plot in Tokyo's Shinjuku quarter, inventively working around existing constructions.

The immaculate curtain walls soar thirty storeys into the sky, with stripes composed of metallic silver parapets and sunblinds. The office tower is nearly 130 metres tall, sharing its plot with a small multipurpose building, a piazza and a garden. The arrangement of the office areas follows the fan-shaped floor plan of the building, which has a total floor area of nearly 85,000 square metres. The open, flexibly organized working areas are located around the curved front; the services are concentrated in the triangular area between the narrow sides of the building. This polarization of functions is no arbitrary formalism but a response to the skyscraper's special location: should NTT employees find their thoughts wandering in the midst of their multimedia pursuits, they can gaze at the view across Shinjuku to the Imperial Palace and the Meji Gardens. From the roof restaurant at the top of the building there is an even better vista: on clear days you can see the snow-capped peak of Mount Fujiyama.

Opposite:

The site is shared with a multipurpose building which joins the main office block by way of a covered walkway, a piazza and garden. The ancillary building is faced by a curved wall of Minnesota stone and is anchored by a vertical volume used for special functions. It is clad in Vermont granite. Minnesota stone is again used at the base of the tower on an open wall which acts to screen a parking lot and entrance and drop-off point for cars.

Right:

The NTT tower reaches 130 metres into the sky and is articulated by alternating bands of aluminium, with a metallic-grey fluoropolymer finish and Kosota stone-clad concrete bands, separated by horizontal windows with projecting protective blinds.

Left:
The stairway in the support building is decorated in tones of dark orange, and offset by a metal staircase which winds around its curved walls. As for the exterior, warm textures contrast with the high-tech sleekness of polished steel.

Opposite top:
Public areas are placed along the curved side of the triangle and overlook the piazza and garden. The floor is marble and the walls covered in laminated silicate calcium board. Lighting is used to articulate the linear patterns used in the reception, and the ceiling is of punched aluminium plate.

Below and opposite:
Floor plans showing the fan-shaped site connected to its semicircular support building. The offices can be organized as open-plan or as enclosed areas. They are situated along the curved front of the tower to take advantage of the panoramic views, whilst the services are concentrated in the narrowing angle of the building.

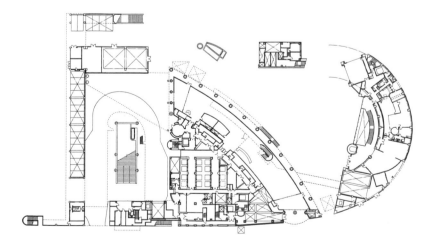

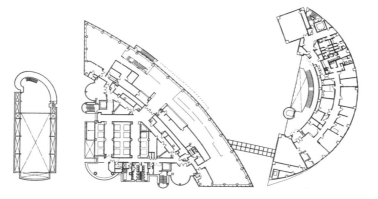

SUVA, BASLE, SWITZERLAND

ARCHITECT:
HERZOG & DE MEURON
1994

When Basle architects Jacques Herzog and Pierre de Meuron were asked to modernize a 1950s office building, their radical solution displayed an unusual respect for the existing structure. They covered it completely with a new mechanized glass and aluminium casing (powered by 900 electrical engines): the old stone building is set at a distance, an indistinct vision glimpsed through the patterned glass panels of the new construction.

The project was designed for a Swiss insurance company (Schweizerische Unfallversicherungsanstalt, or SUVA), which had planned to demolish its old building in order to make way for a larger one. The architects asked permission to leave it standing and add a new wing as an extension. Their glass casing creates an effect of unity which is deliberately offset by the blurred contrast between the old and the new. The building's new outer layer functions like a skin, in practical as well as metaphorical terms. It reacts sensitively to changes in temperature and sunlight and acts as a noise insulator. It also fulfils an important role in terms of corporate image: the company's name is emblazoned on some of the glass panels alongside abstract geometrical patterns.

Computer systems are vital to the work of insurance companies today, and the building's transparent and interactive outer skin offers considerable advantages in this respect. The SUVA building is designed to do without air conditioning. It makes optimal use of daylight – unlike conventional office buildings where sunlight has to be kept out using blinds, which means that computer-compatible lighting systems have to be used even during daylight hours. Art works form an integral part of this architectural design: the works of various contemporary artists can be seen around and inside the building. The project's functional mix includes residential units and a street café alongside the insurance company's offices.

The original stone building of the 1950s office block was retained by the architects and covered by a glass and aluminium casing. Mechanically controlled sections adapt to varying weather conditions and automatically open and close as necessary (*opposite*). Some transparent panels can also be operated manually to control acoustics and insulation.

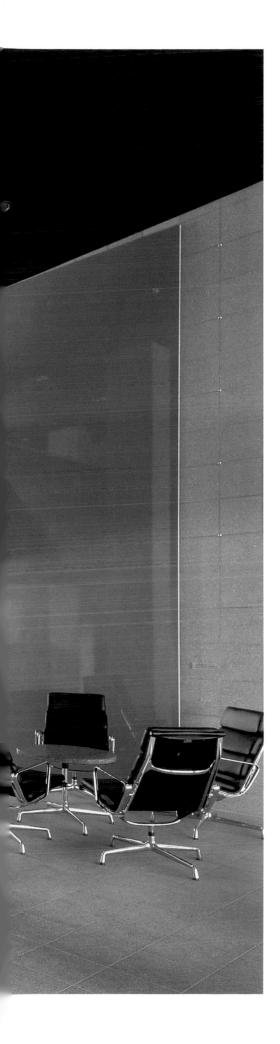

Left:
The reception area is comprised of cool, plain and smooth surfaces. An accent of brilliant colour is added by the orange lacquered panel of Swiss artist Adrian Schiess.

Below:
Ground-floor plan. The site includes offices, residential units and a street café.

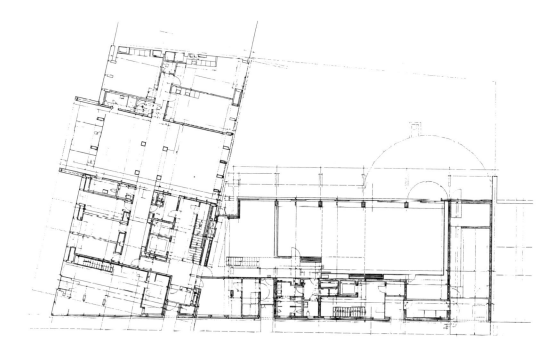

CRÉDIT LYONNAIS,
LILLE, FRANCE

ARCHITECT:
CHRISTIAN DE PORTZAMPARC
1995

Lille, the troubled industrial town in northern France, has moved into the twenty-first century at a single bound. Eurolille, a new commercial district, has been conjured out of nothing around the new railway station for TGV and Eurotunnel express trains. The new quarter is designed to transform the former metropolis of iron and steel into a European centre for the service industries. This giant project is located on a 70-hectare plot close to the city centre. What was once a military parade ground became a showcase for contemporary architecture, in a project pushed through by Lille's mayor (the former Socialist prime minister Pierre Mauroy), and supervised by the radical Dutch architect Rem Koolhaas. Koolhaas reserved the Grand Palais for himself: a complex for exhibitions, conferences and events. Jean Nouvel designed the shopping centre crowned by four residential towers. However, the essential symbol of this urban megaproject, a bulky high-rise block, was designed by Christian de Portzamparc. The L-shaped outline of his 120-metre-high office complex can be seen as a dual reference: it stands both for Lille and for the building's occupant, the

French bank Crédit Lyonnais, which has its regional head office here. "In its unified effect the tower building is an enigmatic, fluctuating presence, which seems to change shape and direction at different times of the day and night. Although it is fixed and stable, it looks as though it could float away" (de Portzamparc).

The massive office building does indeed seem to disappear from view: its shimmering grey-green aluminium and glass casing absorbs and reflects the colours of the sky. The base of the building stands on a complex bridge construction which spans the six glass-covered platforms of the railway station. The technical and EDI departments are located on this raised ground floor; the upper floors house offices and conference rooms. A varied and subtle architectural language distinguished de Portzamparc's previous works; by comparison this unsophisticated high-rise block appears something of a let-down. However, the external appearance is deceptive. The unusual shape allows the architect to create varied interior spaces with bright natural lighting, raising this working environment far above the conventional norm.

Opposite top:
The 120-metre-high grey-green glass and aluminium "L" of de Portzamparc's design stands simultaneously for the Crédit Lyonnais, of which it is the headquarters, and for Lille itself.

Opposite bottom:
The building sits on a complicated bridge foundation which straddles the six platforms of Eurolille railway station.

Opposite right:
Site elevation. The side of the tower which overlooks the city is a giant curtain wall which allows light to pour into the central spaces. The tower itself leans one metre out of the vertical on either side. The entrance to the building is via a curved volume beneath the station canopy.

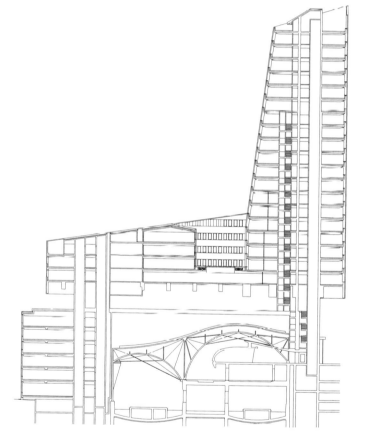

Above:

De Portzamparc wanted to allow as much
light as possible into the office spaces.
Three sides of the building contain large
plate-glass windows in tones which
reflect the maximum glare of sunlight.

Opposite and above:

The entrance hall and lift areas are predominately designed in cool tones, with the addition of small highlights of ochre in the marble terrazzo floor and wooden reception desks. Lighting is recessed and emphasizes key structural components.

INLAND REVENUE, NOTTINGHAM, UK

ARCHITECT:
MICHAEL HOPKINS & PARTNERS
1995

The British Government's decision to move its central tax office to Nottingham was a ray of hope for the economically troubled Midlands city. Thanks to a public outcry, the original design for a faceless office block was abandoned after construction work had started. This meant that the project could benefit the city in architectural as well as economic terms. A competition was held, won by the London architect Michael Hopkins, whose design had several advantages: it could be completed quickly, it combined modernism with vernacular architectural traditions, and it fitted into its context by redeveloping a redundant industrial site. It also presented innovative solutions in terms of environmental awareness and energy efficiency. The site was kept at a low level, to preserve the town's views of Nottingham Castle. It has 43,000 square metres of usable floor space divided among seven separate buildings, three to four storeys high, which are surrounded by tree-lined pathways. Trees and plants are a vital feature of the design, with its internal courtyards and open spaces.

Communal facilities are located centrally in an elegant tent-type construction, with a view across the canal to the castle: these include the staff restaurant, a cafeteria, a nursery, and a fair-sized sports area. Any national tax authority of this size has highly developed electronic networking and data management systems. What distinguishes this Inland Revenue building is its organic integration of architecture and intelligent building management. Striking architectural features also play a vital role in regulating the heat of the building; natural ventilation and air-circulation systems dispense with the need for artificial air-conditioning. For example, the glass-covered staircase towers function like chimneys: in summer they dispose of hot air; in winter they store the warmth from the sun. As well as blinds, the windows have automatically controlled slats inside the triple-glazing which react to changes in daylight. "The environmental design is a simple one, deploying the inherent qualities of the building fabric to modify the environment" (Michael Hopkins).

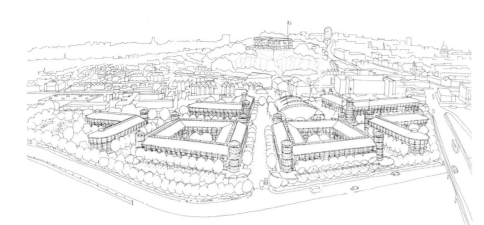

The complex was purposely designed as a sequence of low-level buildings in order not to interrupt views of historic Nottingham and the castle above (see site drawing). Hopkins planned six office blocks with tree-lined walkways between. Between the two building prows facing the canal sits a central canopied structure which houses staff facilities.

Left and below:

The tent-like amenity building is the social heart of the complex. As well as a gymnasium, employees have the benefit of a restaurant, cafeteria and staff nursery. The glass-covered towers housing stairways are an important element of this energy-efficient building. In winter, specially designed glass blocks heat up drums, whilst in summer hot air is drawn from the office spaces and disposed of via the tower lid which can rise by up to 1 metre if necessary.

Opposite top left:

The top-floor open office spaces are ventilated by means of louvres along the central skylight.

Opposite top right:

The northern block is four storeys high. Windows are triple-glazed with automatically controlled blinds, which react to weather conditions, situated in the central panel. Light shelves provide shade from the sun during the day whilst at the same time reflecting light into the interiors, saving on electrical lighting costs. Air is taken in through louvres in the balustrade. Detailing is in harmony with the local architecture which consists of brick and dark grey roofs.

Opposite bottom:

Location plan. The former industrial site is bound on the north side by the canal, to the east by a roadway, and to the south by railway lines.

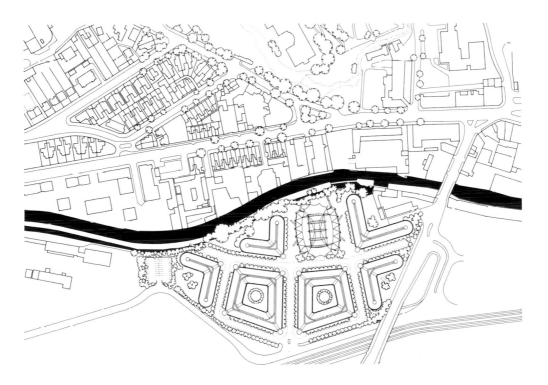

ZENROSAI COMPUTER CENTRE, TOKYO, JAPAN

ARCHITECT/INTERIOR DESIGNER:
DAI'CHI-KOBO ASSOCIATES
1995

Electronic data-processing dominates the day-to-day business of insurance companies. Processing vast quantities of client-related data requires complex software programmes and high-capacity mainframes. The new computer centre of Japanese insurance company Zenrosai was built to bring under one roof all its data-processing departments which had previously operated in various locations.

As well as enhancing the company's operational efficiency, the centre is intended as a vehicle for its corporate image. It is built in three sections. The public wing faces the neighbouring residential area: a low, long gallery pavilion where exhibitions and events are held. A glass passageway functions as a reception area and the connecting link with the huge seven-storey block of the computer and office centre beyond it. Between the parallel wings of the gallery and the office block is a strictly structured, highly intricate architectural landscape: from the entrance side it displays a square bordered by an arcaded stairway; from the other side it features an artificial pool, on the same level as the entrance

lobby. The lavish attention given to areas unconnected with the building's main function, and the elevation of basic materials (bare concrete, steel, wood) follow the canon of Japanese architecture as formulated by architects like Tadao Ando. Tei'chi Takahashi from the Tokyo-based group of architects Dai'chi-Kobo was responsible for the project and does not deny his sources: "I wanted to create a contrast as sharp as possible within the details of the hybrid parts. As for the mixture of structures the material would change according to spatial needs. It was most important that the three structural systems should be well differentiated while at the same time welcoming people as a continuum or sequence."

The Zenrosai Computer Centre has a total floor space of 21,350 square metres. For technical reasons the high-capacity computers are located on the first and second storeys of the office block, while the flexible office spaces, conference and training rooms are on the upper storeys. On the top floor, in penthouse style, is a special restaurant reserved for company executives and VIP guests.

The seven-storeyed computer and office block of the Zenrosai facility rises from its site in a residential suburb of Tokyo. The ceremonial staircase leads to the gallery area, which is a distinct part of the building design.

Opposite:
View towards the entrance hall and the staircase located in the pool.

The gallery has a curved wall with a radius of 100 metres. A ramp runs down to the entrance hall.

Below:

Front and side elevation and site plan. The large computer centre is set back at the rear of the site whilst the gallery block is separated and half-buried in the gently sloping hill. The two parts are connected by the entrance hall and pool.

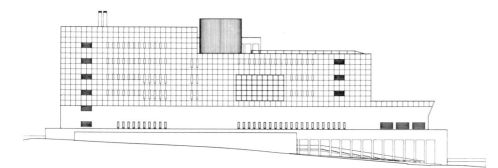

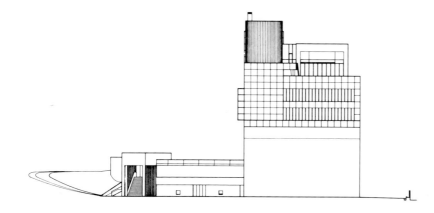

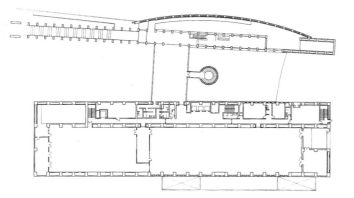

3

HYBRID CONSTRUCTIONS

The "soft" electronic technologies are proving anything but soft in their economic impact. Their development has accelerated the trend towards multifunctional buildings which combine production, administrative, communications and scientific facilities under a single roof. Most of these hybrid constructions use progressive, complex constructional methods and computer-controlled building management systems. They feature the latest glass and façade technologies, temperature-regulation and energy-saving systems. Their progressive technological and environmental qualities are often highlighted as part of a public relations strategy. A striking feature of these buildings is their reclamation of public space. Local government buildings are no longer unapproachable fortresses but services centres in the very best sense: living forums arranged around glazed piazzas, with shops, cafés, information kiosks and events halls which play their part in counteracting the increasing virtualization of everyday life.

ENERGIE-FORUM-INNOVATION, BAD OEYNHAUSEN, GERMANY

ARCHITECT/INTERIOR DESIGNER:
FRANK O. GEHRY & ASSOCIATES
1995

The provincial spa-town of Bad Oeynhausen might seem an unlikely place to have made an original and highly successful contribution to contemporary architecture. It did so through a series of coincidences and the high aspirations of an unconventional client. The local electricity supply company, Elektrizitätswerk Minden-Ravensberg (EMR), had planned to build its new regional network facility on the edge of an industrial wasteland created by the closure of the local steel works. Inspired by Frank O. Gehry's first German project, the Vitra Design Museum, they set their sights as high as they could and invited the famous Californian architect to transform their purpose-built head office into a high-profile architectural attraction. And this was to be more than just a formal experiment: the building was to incorporate all the latest environmental technologies. As consultants, EMR appointed the progressive ecologists from Freiburg's Fraunhofer Institute for Solar Energy Systems. Finally, the company drew up a wide-ranging brief, requiring a combination of office space, conference facilities, exhibition area, electricity supply centre and power station: a challenge that almost surpassed even Gehry's architectural resourcefulness. In fact, this unprecedented mix of functions probably stimulated the architect's creative powers, contributing to the project's success. For in Bad Oeynhausen, Gehry returns to the style of his early, low-budget masterpieces, based on the inherent impressiveness of basic forms and materials: an approach which has become rare in the architect's recent years of prosperity.

The Energie-Forum-Innovation presents a bewildering complex of intersecting buildings, roof extensions and wall sections, surrounded by asphalt pathways; only as you enter and explore the project does its structural logic become clear. The three-storey building has a floor space of 4,500 square metres; it makes optimal use of daylight, especially in the office areas. The main entrance at ground-floor level leads into the building's winding central axis which gives access to

The exhibition hall is set at an angle from the office accommodation behind.

conference rooms, an auditorium and an exhibition area displaying the latest energy-saving products and systems.

The Energie-Forum-Innovation itself takes every opportunity to demonstrate the practical use of advanced ecological technologies: with photoelectric cells on the roof, heat-insulated glass façades, water recycling, computer-controlled temperature regulation, collectors for solar and wind energy, and cooling systems in the ceilings. Rain water is collected in a tank which supplies the lavatory flushing system. The architect's brief also included most of the interior decoration. This made the Bad Oeynhausen complex an architectural showpiece in two respects: a textbook Gehry building complete with his famous cardboard furniture, and a showcase for the very latest systems in energy and resource management.

Left and below:

Gehry has used a mixture of sensuous and contradictory materials to face the main volumes of his building. The plaster-fronted offices stand out in their stark whiteness against the adjacent zinc-clad dining and exhibition areas.

Opposite top left:

Site plan. The building which appears as an incoherent mass of random shapes is bound by the Mindener Strasse and Dehmer Strasse to the south and east, an industrial warehouse area to the west, and a green belt site to the north.

Opposite:

First-, second- and third-floor plans. The building houses an array of different facilities. Offices and technical plant are placed in a linear volume facing the street, occupying two and three levels respectively. The entrance atrium is in the centre of the office block. All other structures are accessible from the atrium and comprise: to the southeast the exhibition hall and a state-of-the-art energy centre; to the north a two-level pavilion with dining area and conference centre. Spaces have been linked by the use of an internal street connecting the public and staff entrances.

South elevation

North elevation

East elevation

West elevation

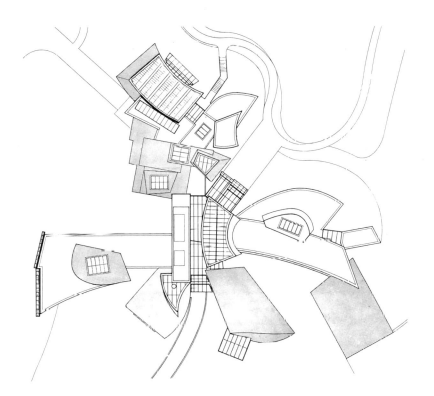

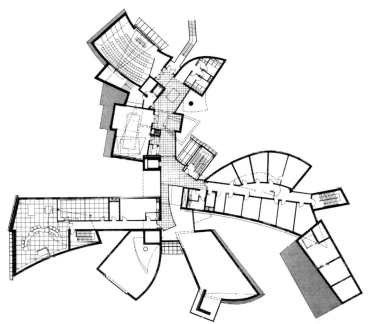

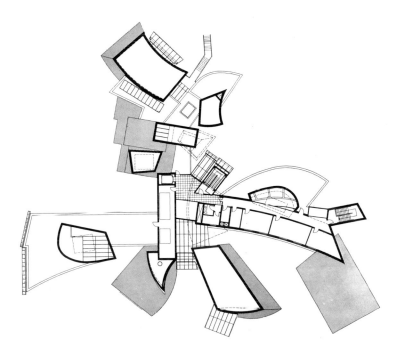

Left:
The exhibition hall is solely devoted to renewable resources, energy conservation and new technologies. This dark and rather cavernous space is lined with laminated timber beams. The windows are situated at either end in thermal storage walls.

Opposite top:
Gehry has made his design a showcase for "green" architecture, adopting energy-saving devices such as natural ventilation and daylighting. His play of material and colour is again evident in the plain white plaster walls and the rich earth colours of the wooden office-dividers in the energy-control centre.

Opposite bottom:
The auditorium for company and public presentations overlooks the Werre Valley and neighbouring mountains and is lit by natural light diffused from above.

ASTRA HÄSSLE, GOTHENBURG, SWEDEN

ARCHITECT:
WINGÅRDH ARKITEKTKONTOR
1995–97

In 1989 the Swedish pharmaceuticals company Astra Hässle, part of the Wallenberg industrial conglomerate, announced a restricted competition for the extension of its research buildings in Gothenburg. Gert Wingårdh, the winner, was relatively young; although he had caught the eye of the architectural world with a series of smaller projects, he had no previous experience of large-scale commercial building. Perhaps this explains his unconventional approach: he was the only competitor to present the new facilities not as a separate block but as a diffuse amplification of the existing site.

Astra Hässle opted for this nonconformist design and the first section of the building, completed in 1995, has proved a magnificent vindication of their choice. What is more,

from above, the new aluminium-covered sections give structure and coherence to the whole.

The extensive complex, which includes laboratories, conference centres and a cafeteria, will cover a total of 70,000 square metres by the time it is completed in 1997. Over 1,000 employees work in the pharmaceutical, biological and medical research departments. All the current safety precautions for highly sensitive scientific activities have been observed, and the individual departments meet all the requirements of clean-room environments: nonetheless, the building's interior conveys an impression of democratic openness and accessibility. This places it squarely, and unexpectedly, in the Scandinavian modernist tradition.

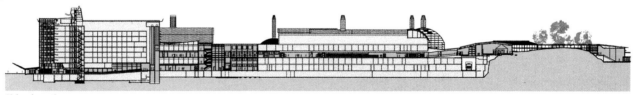

Side elevation

the superstitious belief that contemporary buildings need to stand alone to have their full impact is impressively refuted by Wingårdh's technoid structure, which dynamically overlays the barren brick landscape of the original site, forging a new design from the juxtaposition of old and new. Seen

Participation and dialogue were central to this exceptional project even at the planning stage: ten working parties of employees met regularly to discuss the architects' proposals, defining the form and furnishings of their future working environment down to the last detail.

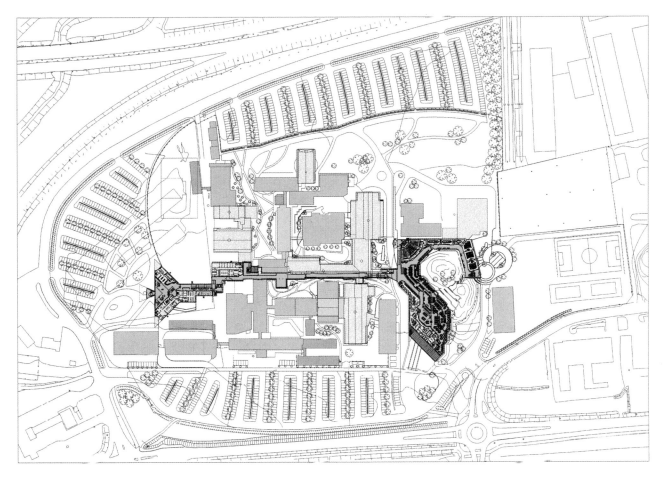

Above:

Wingårdh has created an aluminium-coated spine to house the new research facility for the Swedish pharmaceutical firm Astra, which is accommodated within the existing industrial fabric.

Below right:

The use of light-reflective aluminium was an attempt to maximize daylight in a heavily built-up complex where the majority of the old buildings are constructed of dark brick.

Below left:

Section through a typical laboratory block. The arched roof permits a low eave whilst still allowing for 1 or 1 ½ plant rooms which was an important consideration given the height restrictions imposed.

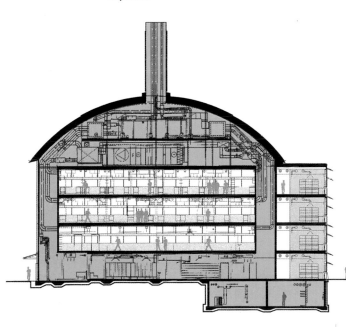

Above:

Glazed façade and detail of one of the laboratory wings. All glass is protected by a continuous perforated and slightly curved aluminium sheet. The glass is also naturally coated to reduce solar glare.

Opposite:

The staff canteen can seat 70 per cent of the employees at any one time, an ideal opportunity for social interaction. Acoustics are important: all tables are coated underneath with dampening material, walls are not parallel, and a sound-proofing course has been added behind the aluminium ceiling. The glass partitions were designed by the artist Peder Josefsson.

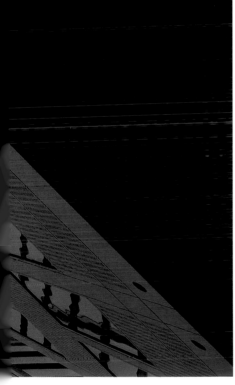

STADHUS,
THE HAGUE, THE NETHERLANDS

ARCHITECT:
RICHARD MEIER & PARTNERS
1995

Residents of The Hague have nicknamed their new city hall the "Witte Gigant", the White Giant. This complex, built on a wedge-shaped plot, is the largest building created by New York architect Richard Meier to date: it is some 250 metres long, with a total floor space of 120,000 square metres, forming the centrepiece of the city's ambitious urban renovation programme.

This city hall is no anonymous administrative colossus but a unique, democratically structured area which combines a broad range of functions: it is a setting for public events and a pleasant place for a stroll. Two long wings fan out gently from the centre of the building to the east and the west, accommodating 2,300 local government employees. In between them is a breathtaking interior space, the glass atrium: 47 metres high and the largest covered square in Europe, easily big enough to hold either Milan's Galleria Vittorio Emmanuele or the Piazza San Marco of Venice. For the architect this superlative has symbolic force: "This Citizens' Hall forms the new res publica" (Meier). Even after office hours, life continues here with a vast array of different events. The main entrance stands opposite two eminent arts buildings of recent times: the Nederlands Dans Theater by Rem Koolhaas to the left and the Theater Het Spui by Herman Hertzberger to the right. The eastern tip of the Stadhus houses the municipal library and archive, along with a privately run furniture shop; the western end is reserved for commercial offices.

The project was completed nearly ten years after Meier won the design competition in 1986. The delay is due to the architect's tenacity: he brought work to a halt when financial crises and government cutbacks jeopardized his expensive façade, with its enamelled porcelain panels. Meier's persistence paid off: his white giant has survived in all its immaculate glory. This obstinate purist also fought successfully on two other counts. An outdoor staircase leads from the Registry Office to a "city" window cut deep into the southern façade, where newly married couples can have their photograph taken against the splendid backdrop of the historic Hague. Meier also ensured that all public areas were kept free of supplementary art works, to preserve the full impact of his design. Only in the council chamber did Meier allow a single bronze bust: that of the Queen of The Netherlands.

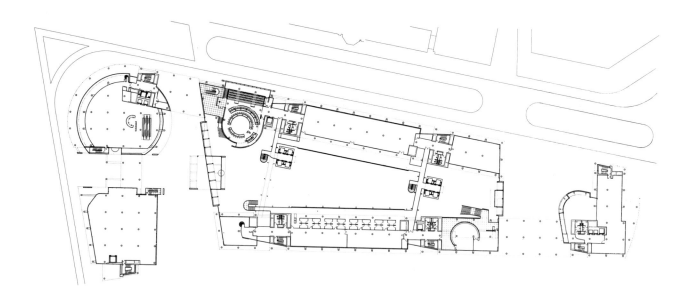

Opposite:
Plan of level one. The City Hall complex, measuring 244 x 76 metres, includes a semicircular public library in the north-west corner, faced across a public piazza by the Council Chamber. The main horizontal office arms, comprising 10–12 storeys, diverge from each other at an angle of 10.5 degrees.

Top right:
Detail of the façade of City Hall reflected in a neighbouring building. Meier has unified diverse facilities by cladding the whole in bands of a unique aluminium glazing system with 40mm mullions.

Below:
Meier's largest public building is a major contribution to the regeneration of the centre of The Hague. The wedge-shaped complex sits next to the recent theatre buildings by Rem Koolhaas and Herman Hertzberger.

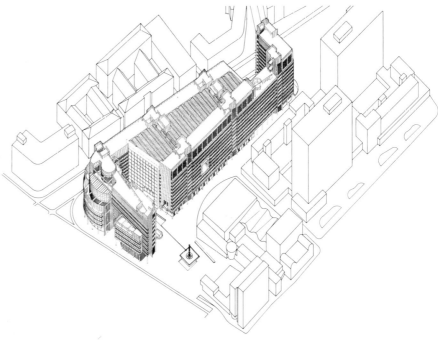

Top left:

The Council Chamber is lined with 85 x 100cm porcelain enamelled metal panels.

Below:

The main library is of a conventional design. Open spaces throughout are in reinforced concrete, also faced with enamelled metal panels.

Opposite:

The 14-storey-high atrium or Citizens' Hall acts as a modern-day forum. The glass roof is supported by free-standing laminated timber trusses. The aerial bridges, the elevator, and stair cones are of white-painted steel.

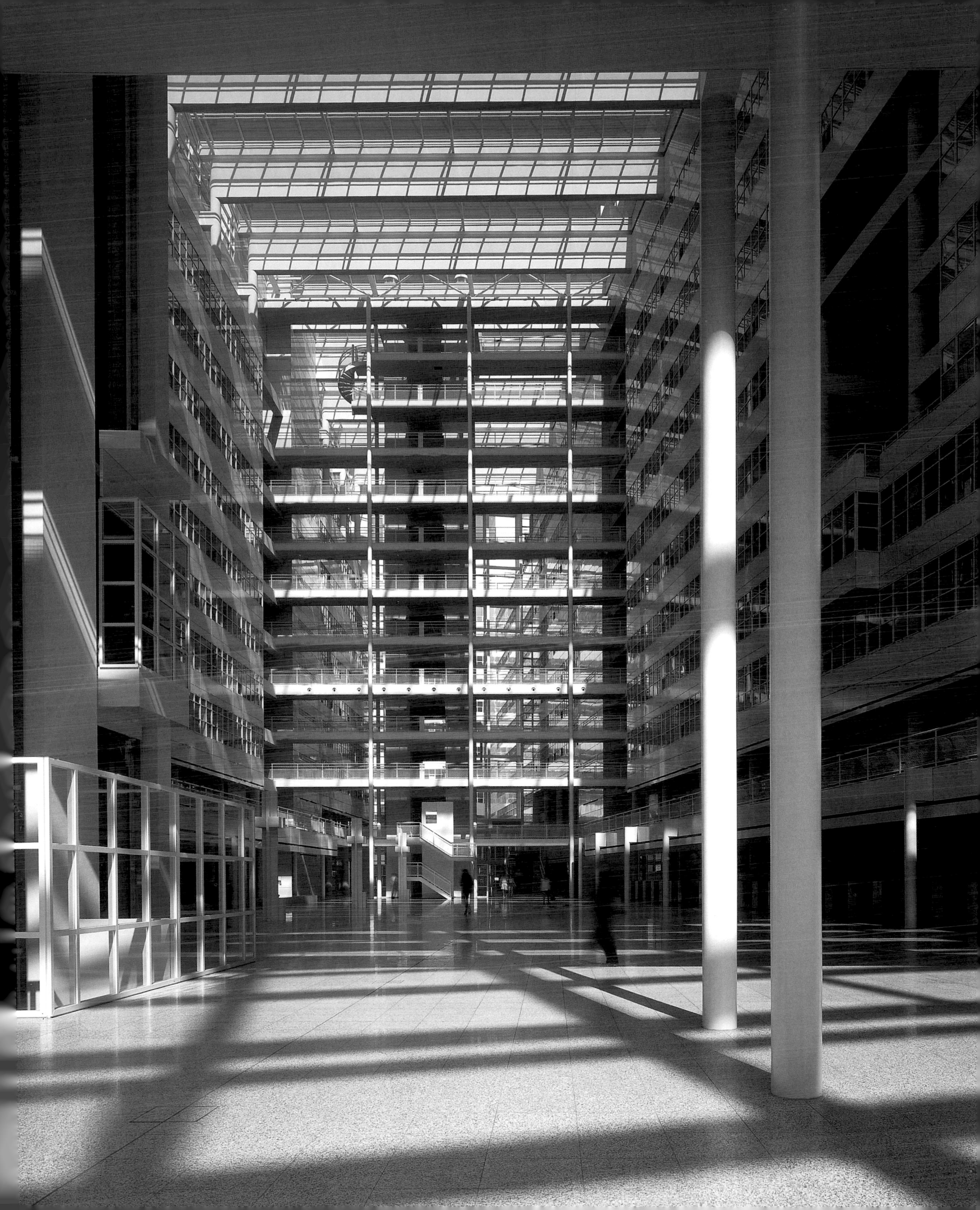

NEUE MESSE,
LEIPZIG, GERMANY

ARCHITECT:
VON GERKAN, MARG & PARTNER
1996

Germany is the undisputed world leader in the international trade fair business: in no other country do so many large-scale, highly equipped exhibition centres compete for the custom of industries and visitors. This did not deter Leipzig, a traditional trade fair city since it was granted a licence during the Holy Roman Empire in 1248, from boldly relaunching its activities in this sector following the collapse of the Communist régime. The old exhibition centre, which had done duty for the past forty years, was abandoned. A new exhibition and conference complex was built on the site of a former airport outside the city: it was completed in the record time of only three years, at a cost of over DM 1.3 billion (£0.53 billion).

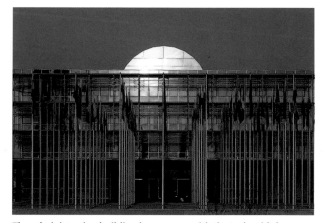

The administration building keeps pace with the technoid shapes of the Messe complex.

Compared with competitors like Hanover and Frankfurt its dimensions are relatively modest: a built-up area of 272,300 square metres, with 102,500 square metres of exhibition space. However, the Neue Messe is exceptional for its design, created by the successful Hamburg architects Von Gerkan, Marg & Partner. A central glass hall was designed in collaboration with London-based specialist Ian Ritchie, serving as both an entrance hall and the main axis of the complex. The hall is 250 metres long; its arched roof – 80 metres wide and 30 metres high – bears comparison with the legendary iron and glass constructions of the nineteenth

century, displaying the very best of contemporary engineering skills. The exhibition halls, conference centre and administrative buildings are arranged on either side of this huge glass passageway, which uses the minimum of heat-regulating equipment. Within it are a reception area, shops and restaurants. "Constructional detail should serve the architectural style of the building as a whole": this was the motto of architect Volkwin Marg, who supervised the project. Service pipes and the cabling for the multimedia network are hidden from view: the chimneys of the heating plant are disguised as a high-tech campanile.

The city authorities were not satisfied with commissioning only the architect: the Neue Messe also features a series of twenty-five substantial art installations by different contributors. Participants include German artists like Rosemarie Trockel and Günther Förg alongside international stars such as Sol LeWitt and Jenny Holzer. The latter laconically placed the following, very apt observation in a neon sign over the entrance ticket desks: "Money creates taste".

The glass and steel hall is a masterpiece of engineering. Glass panels without any visible means of support are held aloft as if by magic. In reality the panels are kept in place at nodal points. The spaceframe is a self-loading shell, stabilized by additional tie vaults every 25 metres. Tones are deliberately monochromatic to emphasize the colourfulness of the people within and the events taking place. Warm and natural materials are used only at points of human contact, such as shell lime instead of artificial stone on the stairways of the glass hall, and wood in the handrails of the parapets.

Right:

The 80m-high steel-framed tower serves a dual purpose. It advertises the Leipzig Messe logo, whilst at the same time acting as a chimney for the heating plant below.

Opposite top:

Passageways are constructed as glazed tubes.

Opposite bottom:

Atrium in the conference building with spiral staircase and colourful artwork by Hanno Otten.

SCIENCE PARK,
GELSENKIRCHEN, GERMANY

ARCHITECT:
KIESSLER + PARTNER
1995

The Gelsenkirchen Wissenschaftspark (Science Park) stands on the site of a disused steelworks in Germany's Ruhr region – an area which has been hard hit by the decline of heavy industry. The project was intended as a forward-looking architectural and commercial enterprise, a signal that this region is heading for the new age of "soft technologies". Architect Uwe Kiessler based his design on a grand symbolic gesture, making prominent use of the new technology. The 300-metre-long glass front rises at an angle from the shores of an artificial lake; the lower third of its large-format façade sections can be raised during the summer. The glass-covered walkway at the front gives access to the new offices and workshops set back from the entrance. The science park has over 700 employees in new industries, including photo-electric technology, cable communications, neuro-fuzzy technologies and the new media. It was financed by the state of Nordrhein-Westfalen: its experimental combination of subsidized infrastructure and private enterprise may well prove a model to be emulated elsewhere. The new industries have been heralded as a dynamic force which could revitalize

Europe's ageing industrial landscape: this project is designed to promote their development through its combination of information-sharing, cooperative research and entrepreneurial freedom.

The architecture points the way to the future: "The design of the complex was intended to symbolize technical competence and hope for the future. Architectural developments of the future will mainly affect the surfaces of buildings. Their outer layer will become ever more complex, responding to varying environmental conditions with increasing sophistication" (Uwe Kiessler). The building's temperature- and energy-management systems are supplemented by its own solar power station on the roof, where rows of silicon cells produce around two million kilowatt hours annually. The Wissenschaftspark is also a showpiece exhibit in the International Building Exhibition taking place in the Ruhr region until 1998. One of the central themes of this major event is "Work in the Park". The crystal palace of Gelsenkirchen translates this metaphor into a convincing reality.

Opposite top:
The Science Park is one of the main projects in the Emscher Park International Architectural Exhibition. The 300-metre-long glass face rises at an angle from an artificial lake.

Opposite bottom:
Behind the glazed wall is a walkway beyond which office blocks and workshops have been placed at right angles in a "comb" formation.

Below:
Cross-section with adjoining office blocks.

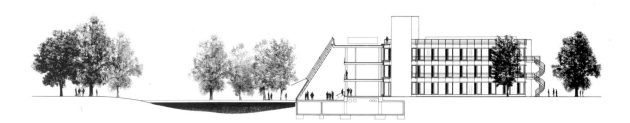

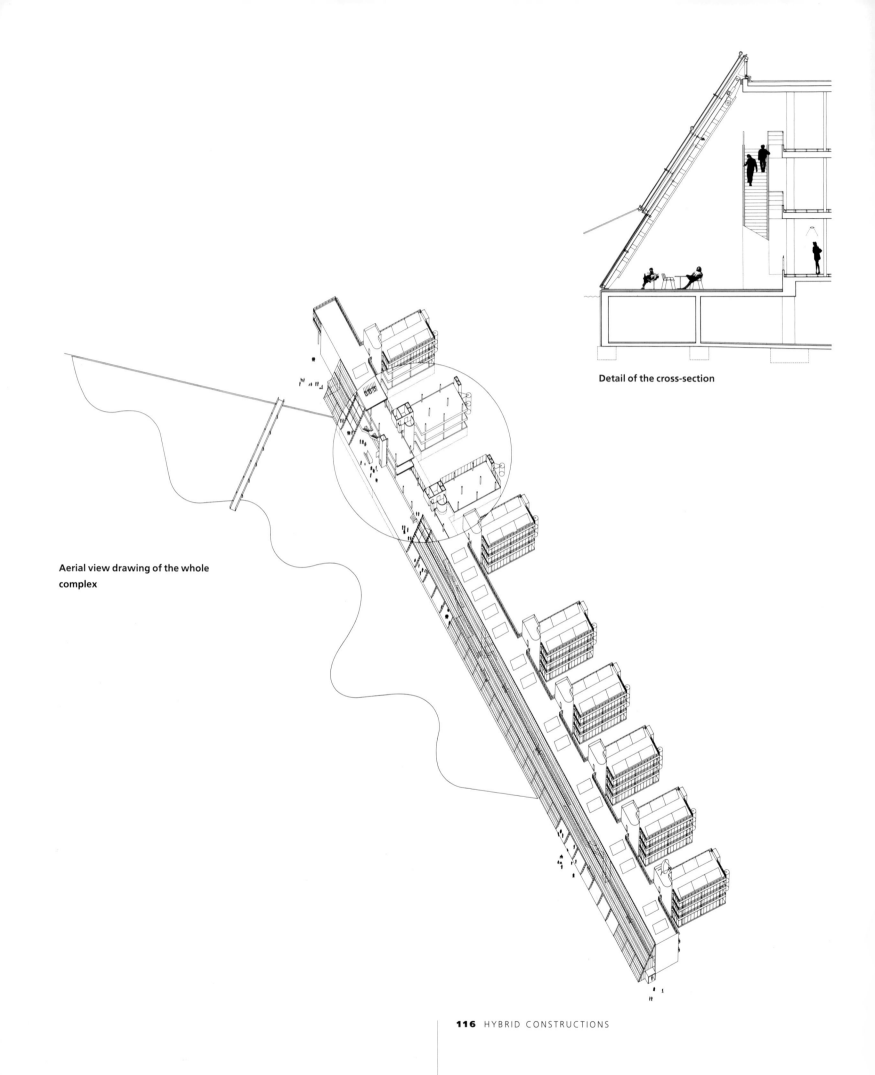

Detail of the cross-section

Aerial view drawing of the whole
complex

Kiessler's design shows a remarkable emphasis on angularity and linearity reinforced by an absence of colour and needless detail.

HÔTEL DU DÉPARTEMENT
DES BOUCHES-DU-RHÔNE,
MARSEILLES, FRANCE

ARCHITECT:
ALSOP & STÖRMER
INTERIOR DESIGNER:
ALSOP & STÖRMER,
ANDRÉE PUTMAN/ECART INTERNATIONAL
1994

In their design for the new local government building of the French département of Bouches-du-Rhône, the Anglo-German team Alsop & Störmer sought to create a striking piece of contemporary architecture which would transport the magic blue of the Côte d'Azur into the desolate outskirts of Marseilles. Their design was selected from 156 competition entrants because it presented a solution that was both commercially viable and visually impressive. "Simple, low-cost technologies have been utilized to create a highly sophisticated relationship between the internal and external environments" (William Alsop).

The complex consists of three parallel buildings, 150 to 160 metres in length, providing a total floor space of 93,500 square metres. Between the two blocks of offices ("L'Administratif") is a glass atrium which functions as an entrance area for the public: a piazza with shops, cafés, a media library, a sports centre and a nursery. A two-storey roof extension crowns the taller of the administrative buildings: this airship-penthouse is reserved for top-level administrative functions and the departmental president's separate restaurant. The complex is completed by the "Délibératif": a cigar-shaped high-tech construction which houses the large assembly hall and conference rooms.

Paris designer Andrée Putman was responsible for the interior design of all the public areas: her sparse and elegant style complements the sober expressiveness of the architecture. The project was designed for optimum response to environmental changes, keeping energy consumption to the minimum. The building management system uses roof sensors (which measure temperature, light and wind levels) to control sun blinds and ventilation shutters, warm and cool water-piping systems in the floors, and the central air-conditioning system (used mainly in the conference wing).

Opposite bottom:
Nicknamed "Le Grand Bleu", the complex of the Hôtel du Département consists of three parallel buildings. Two office blocks (one surmounted by a two-storey roof extension) are connected by a glass atrium. A third, flattened cylindrical structure houses the assembly hall and conference rooms.
Opposite top:
The cigar-shaped wing is sheltered by mobile textile sun-shades.

Below:
Section: the building contains council chambers, restaurants, a library, media centre, sports centre, offices, a crèche, a visitors' centre and parking.

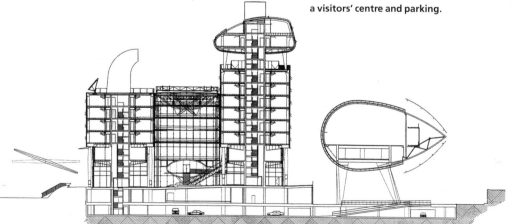

Above:

Glazed futuristic walkways connect the administration building with the conference centre.

Opposite:

The reception area was conceived to redress the usual situation in institutional buildings where a number of small, badly serviced and uncomfortable waiting-rooms are gathered around a small central area. Alsop envisaged a light and cheerful plaza with magazine stands and coffee shops. In the main area, concrete, steel and glass have retained a bright and simple appearance. The large X struts are both functional and decorative and are used internally and externally.

THE COMPASS CENTRE, HEATHROW AIRPORT, UK

ARCHITECT:
NICHOLAS GRIMSHAW AND PARTNERS
INTERIOR DESIGNER:
AUKETT ASSOCIATES
1994

A substantial commercial project right next to one of the world's largest airports has to fulfil very particular requirements: the safety of the radar system and the air traffic it controls must not be impaired. The design by high-tech specialist Nicholas Grimshaw, built on the edge of London's Heathrow Airport, exhibits this hyperfunctionality in all its features. The complex of three interconnected buildings is 188 metres long with a total floor space of 22,300 square metres. It is only three storeys high, enabling it to remain invisible on radar screens despite its size. This invisibility is achieved without the expensive "stealth" materials which the defence industry uses to absorb radar waves: instead the ingenious façade design uses rounded and sloping sections of glass and aluminium to diffuse the radar waves, while the outward-sloping long sides of the building direct them towards the surrounding car-park areas where they are absorbed by the paving and parked vehicles. At night, the impressive sun-shades on the building serve to conceal all interior lighting which could distract planes as they land or take off.

The building complex, which cost an estimated £17 million, would have had to incorporate these and other safety features even if it had not been let to British Airways. As it is, the airline has made this unique building into the control centre for its global network and an operational centre for flight crews departing from Heathrow. These are the bare statistics: every day the new Compass Centre coordinates nearly 1,000 flights worldwide; in addition to its fixed workforce nearly 3,000 crew members pass through it daily. Alongside the work areas and staff accommodation, the building has shops, canteens, a medical centre and a hairdresser. For all the sophistication of the architecture, sadly the interior decoration fails to transcend the conventional airport banalities.

Opposite:

Using geometry rather than radar-absorbent material, waves are reflected off the sloped, glazed panels which lean out at an angle of 21 degrees, and are then deflected into the car park.

Below:

The façade is clad in various forms of glass and aluminium. The internal staircases can be seen through glazed block walls designed to shine like beacons at night. The blue horizontal aluminium louvres give the impression of blue skies even on grey days. The aerofoil shape reduces their radar impact.

Bottom:

Hidden shine of the Compass Centre. In order not to confuse incoming aircraft, specially constructed anti-dazzle panels have been fitted to the roof to prevent light glare upwards.

Opposite top:

Elevation showing the arrangement of three blocks serviced independently. Each has a glass atrium and glass links between. Grimshaw's design for the British Airways Combined Operation Centre, where more than 350,000 flights per year are controlled, has been heralded as the first "stealth" building in Britain.

Below:

Site plan. The building is situated next to Heathrow Airport between the Northern Perimeter Road and the Bath Road, and consists of three volumes, Westpoint, Meridian and Eastpoint, connected by walkways.

Opposite left:

The communal areas of the interiors were designed to encourage interactivity. The spiral staircase which links the three floors is surrounded by transparent landings, escalators and lifts.

Opposite centre right:

The three blocks are connected by glazed walkways bridging all floors.

Opposite bottom:

Façade and detail of contrasting colours and materials.

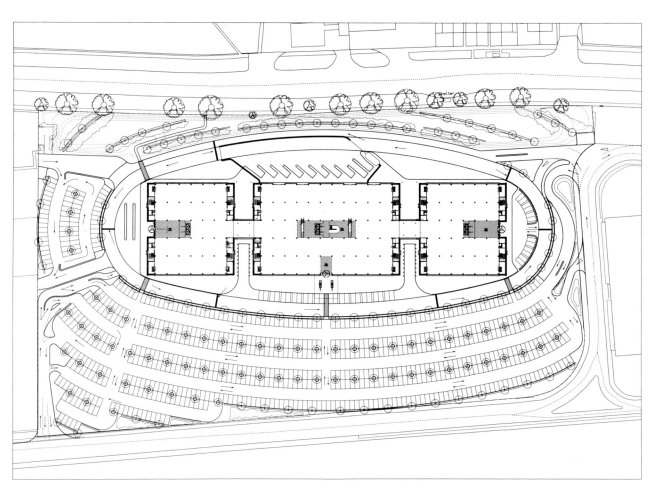

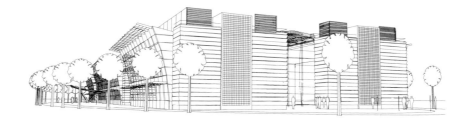

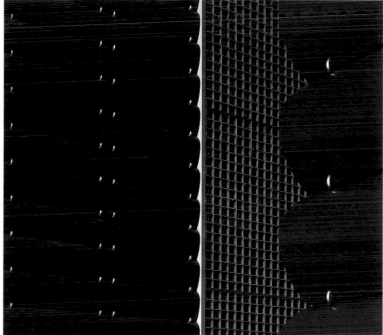

SYSTEM SOLUTION CENTRE TOCHIGI, UTSUNOMIYA, JAPAN

ARCHITECT/INTERIOR DESIGNER:
ARCHITECT 5 PARTNERSHIP
1995

A new Information Park, designed to bring the industries of the communications age to the province of Tochigi, is being created on undeveloped pastureland outside Utsunomiya. Its pilot project was the System Solution Centre Tochigi (SSCT): a testing centre for new hardware and software products, where final modifications are made before products are launched. SSCT was completed in 1995 with a capacity of 500 computers, making it the largest facility of this type in Japan to date.

This joint venture (funded by state, local government and private investors) sets standards in architectural as well as technological terms, providing a model for the projected extension of the Information Park. The airy, transparent pavilion made of steel and glass (96 metres long and 29 metres wide) fits snugly into its natural setting, with minimal environmental impact. The building's main architectural features combine to create an impression that it is suspended in mid-air. The pavilion rests on the pillars of the underground car park; its long front overlooks the sloping site, bordered by an artificial lake (this leads into a stream which runs across the large open space of the meadowland plot). On the other side of the building, an elegant footbridge connects the upper storey to a public footpath on higher ground. The architects decided to locate the load-bearing pillars on the outside of the building, in front of the glass façade: on the inside this gave them a highly flexible, adaptable internal space; on the outside it enabled them to create a brilliantly unpretentious high-tech variant of the classical veranda.

The building's two entrances ensure that the testing areas and public areas are kept separate. The ground floor is reached by a bridge across the water: this is where the scientists work and where specialist training courses are held. Another bridge leads to the upper storey, which has a restaurant, a relaxation area and an exhibition area, all of which are open to the general public. The roof terrace with its wooden floors provides a public sundeck for anyone wanting to take a break from the stresses of the computer world.

Opposite top:
The ground floor of the building is raised slightly above ground level, which gives the impression that the building is floating over the surrounding hill slope. The curves of the roof further soften the construction and give it a geomorphic compatibility.

Opposite bottom:
Sundeck for high-tech venturers. The roof pavilion is also accessible to the general public.

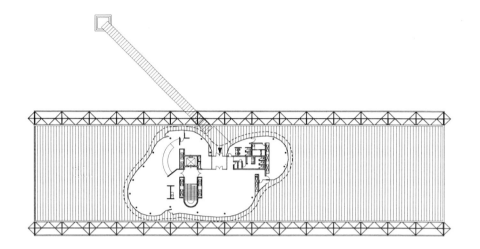

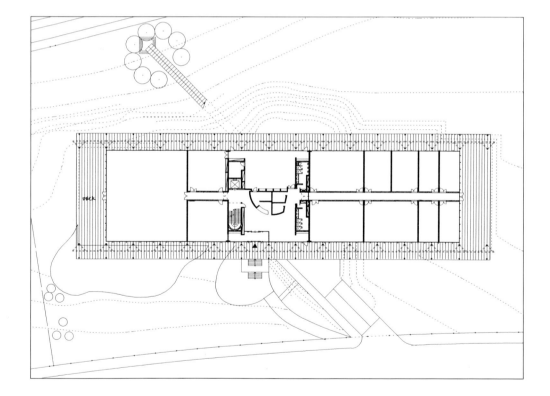

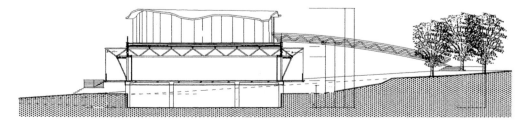

Top left:

The upper floor contains the staff amenities and a seminar and show room. The
restaurant, kitchen, relaxation room
and roof terrace all have views into the
surrounding landscape.

Centre left:

Ground-floor plan. The space can be
adapted by the use of movable partitions.

Bottom left:

East-west section. The restaurant can be
reached by a footbridge which leads from
the neighbouring hillside.

Opposite:

The two façades. Aluminium pipes along
the eaves act as louvres and are a modern
equivalent of traditional Japanese
wooden structures. The building in fact is
conceived along the lines of a vernacular
Japanese building: interior, veranda,
eaves and exterior. This is accentuated
by the use of ornamental rocks and a
tranquil water feature.

RITE,
KEIHANNA, JAPAN

ARCHITECT/INTERIOR DESIGNER:
NIKKEN SEKKEI
1993

In the hilly area between the towns of Osaka, Kyoto and Nara is the Japanese science city of Keihanna, designed as a high-technology and research location for companies and public institutions. RITE (Research Institute for Innovative Technology for the Earth) was founded as a national organization in 1990 and established its first large-scale laboratory complex here.

From the outset the project was intended as an experiment in environmentally-friendly, energy-efficient architecture. Project architects Nikken Sekkei were commissioned "to design a highly functional, modern laboratory building by employing the conventional architectural know-how which has been elaborated in Japan since ancient times to adapt buildings to the Japanese climate". The L-shaped complex, with a total floor space of 6,900 square metres, is embedded in the gently sloping plot. Most of the laboratories are in the basement. The upper storeys house offices, a conference area, the library and a cafeteria. The modern-looking design of the cylindrical atrium and the wide barrel roofs of the two wings have their roots in traditional Japanese architecture. Their deep sloping surfaces protect the building from the bright summer sun and also collect large quantities of rainwater, which is stored in a tank and fed into the water recycling system. A large array of solar batteries on the atrium tower contributes to the building's energy supply. The double roof construction, a system of cold-water pipes, and a wind tunnel which runs through the building, combine to create an energy-efficient heating and ventilation system. The building's consumption of primary energy for heating and ventilation purposes is one third lower than in comparable conventional buildings.

Below:

Eastern façade. The dramatically sloping profile is based on traditional Japanese building practice evolved to cope with the local climate of high rainfall, and strong sunlight in summer. This glazed volume houses a reception atrium, staff amenities and conference facilities. The lower barrel-vaulted structure is used as a laboratory space. It is half buried in the ground and topped with a double-skin roof which preserves a stable ambient temperature.

Right:

Section elevation showing the ventilation channel to the left and the reservoir for storing rainwater to the right. The main atrium is flanked by the laboratory block and research facilities.

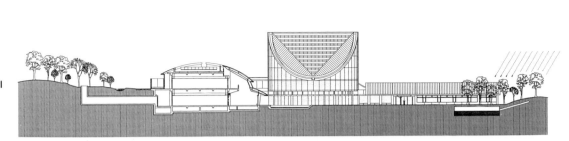

Opposite:

The building houses facilities for research into and development of new technologies to balance the growth of industries with the preservation of global resources. As such, the complex was designed to make the maximum use of energy-saving devices. The roof of the atrium tower is topped with a sun-power generating device. The complex has a self-supporting air-conditioning system. Reclaimed rainwater is circulated around the building from a spring, via a shallow brook and a waterfall, to a pool. Cleaned by stones in the pool, it is also used as a non-potable water supply.

Left:

Multipurpose space in the atrium. Indirect light from the glazed walls filters into this area through opaque glass panels. The use of wood lends a human dimension which contrasts with the high-tech appearance of the research facilities.

TELEFÓNICA DE ESPAÑA, MADRID, SPAIN

ARCHITECT:
FRANCISCO JOSÉ LARRUCEA
1995

The new complex of Spain's largest telecommunications company combines two functions: it is both a national data-processing centre and Madrid's central telephone exchange. A densely built-up industrial area in the city's suburbs was not perhaps the most desirable location, and a restrained style of architecture would hardly have been appropriate for the setting. Francisco José Larrucea's design makes a bold statement within its disparate context. Behind a cylindrical office building is a group of three huge silver blocks which house the company's high-capacity computer systems; at the end stands an 80-metre-high radio tower. The three closed containers form a deliberate contrast to the transparent circular building, signalling the different functions of these high-tech facilities. All activities based on personal interaction and communication are concentrated in the office cylinder; beyond this is the realm of technicians and engineers. "Habitats for machines and their operators, modern and sophisticated workshops for the meeting of machine and man. These spaces were designed as an ever-lasting, efficient and silent container in counterpoint to the lively, articulated spaces for people intended to express a relation with the outside world" (Larrucea).

Madrid's new central Telefónica complex has a total floor space of nearly 62,000 square metres; forty per cent of this is accounted for by two vast underground storeys, which cover the entire length of the site. This electronic nerve centre of Spanish telecommunications has understandably stringent security regulations, with strict limits on public access. Most clients and visitors get no further than the entrance level of the round reception building, which has conference rooms, an exhibition area, a computer club and a cafeteria alongside the reception and security checkpoint.

Top left:
The transparent handling of the exterior of the office block contrasts with the stark silver volume of the buildings housing the machinery. Enclosed entirely along three sides, they are relieved only by a continuous band of windows in the passageways which run east to west. To the rear can be seen one of the various routes which link the office building with the System Development structure.

Top right:
The use of simple forms and materials and the predominant colours of light grey, metallic grey and green give the complex a timeless quality. The design plays on a dialogue between volume and space in which the areas between the buildings take the place of a fifth, "invisible" form.

Bottom left:
The internal stairwell is lined with concrete. Light enters through studded panels with opaque glass inserts. As with the main forms, Larrucea has experimented with geometrical shapes and materials; the hardness of the zig-zag industrial metal staircase contrasts with the softness of the diffused light and the smoothness of the walls.

Bottom right:
Basement circulation area. The ceilings are of anodized aluminium mesh. Light filters in from the glazed upper level.

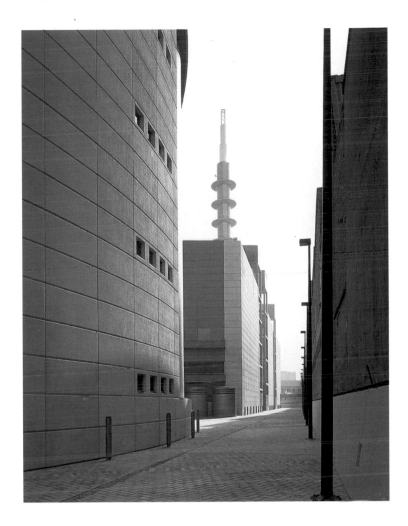

Opposite:

Reception and lobby area of the office block. The flooring is in PVC sections streaked in various shades of grey. Warmth is given to these predominantly cold and metallic communal areas by the use of ochre wall panels and recessed downlighters, which give off a patterned lighting effect. The ceiling has specially designed sound-absorbent panels with aluminium inserts. The doors are in fire-resistant blue-grey steel sheet with a Firestop glass view panel.

Right:

Axonometric and ground-floor plan. The CNIT serves both as the Spanish Telecom national data-processing head-quarters centre and as Madrid's central telephone exchange. Facilities are housed in four main blocks. A cylindrical office building stands in front of three volumes which contain the computer amenities. An 80-metre-high telecommunications tower surmounts the longest of these buildings. Below ground, two basement levels stretch beneath the whole site.

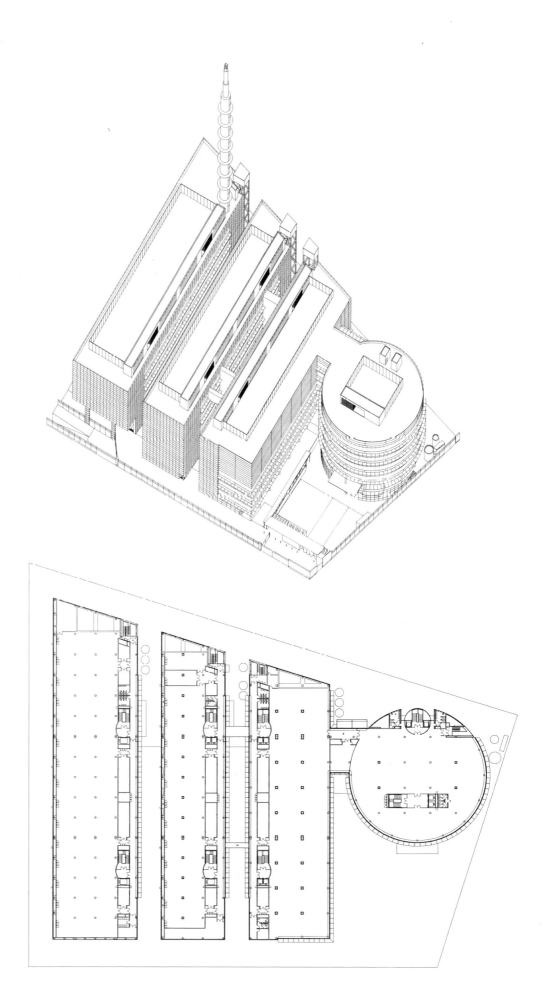

MOTOROLA CUSTOMERS' CENTER, SCHAUMBURG, USA

INTERIOR DESIGNER:
HOLABIRD & ROOT
1994

Customer orientation could hardly be called a new concept among the strategic watchwords of modern corporations, yet few have taken it as far as electronics company Motorola in its Customers' Center for Systems Integration, completed in 1994. Here, the purchasers of highly complex communications systems are welcomed in the selfsame building where these systems are finally assembled and tested.

The new unit, combining a production facility and a client centre, was created by converting an ordinary factory building (with an area of 3,900 square metres) in the middle of Motorola's huge industrial complex. It is designed to receive high-level clients: representatives of governments and large organizations, technical directors of industrial groups and public authorities, whose commissions can be worth hundreds of millions of dollars. Here, the members of this exclusive clientèle (which nonetheless represents over

1,000 visitors per year) can witness in person the last test phases of the systems they have ordered. "The space mixes industry and customers, which are typically kept separate. So we designed ways to make smooth transitions in all areas, from the parking lot to reception, then into the actual testing sites", explains project architect Tod Desmarais, from the Chicago company Holabird & Root, outlining the particular challenge of this project. The offices of client advisers as well as meeting and presentation rooms are located near to the visitor entrance. From here a steel ramp leads into the factory hall, where the various production islands are arranged in honeycomb fashion, set at an angle to the floor plan. The client trail is marked out with white floor tiles. Even the most high-flying guests have to make a concession to factory realities: everyone has to wear PVC protective goggles while they inspect the latest in communications technology.

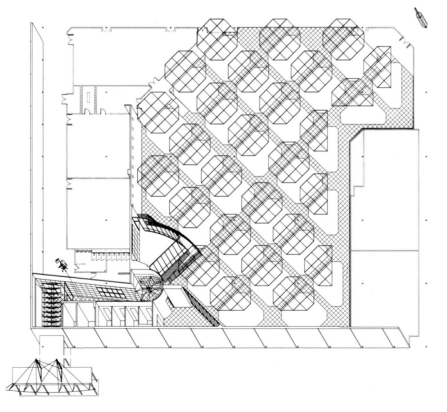

Opposite:

Floor plan illustrating the grid-like pattern of the factory floor, as well as the relatively small area used for the all-important contact with clients.

Above:

The lobby in the form of a rotunda is covered by a metal and glass shallow-domed canopy. A glass doorway leads to testing and assembly facilities.

Left and opposite:
The smaller of two conference rooms is set above the factory floor which it overlooks through glazed walls. From the comfort of their chairs, clients can watch their custom-made products being assembled and tested.

Below:
The factory floor is organized in a modular grid. A white-tiled walkway leads visitors to the closer inspection of the assembly lines.

SYSTEMS RESEARCH DEPARTMENT, SEIBERSDORF, AUSTRIA

ARCHITECT:
COOP HIMMELBLAU
1995

The Austrian Research Centre is an extensive complex of scientific buildings located at Seibersdorf near Vienna. Its decision to build a new office block was prompted by the creation of a new department combining various disciplines (Systems Research in Technology, Economy and Environment). An empty 1960s warehouse stood on the proposed site: no-one would have raised the slightest objection to its demolition. No-one but the architects, that is. Coop Himmelblau's tireless avant-gardists maintain that the dynamics of architectural change should be a vital and visible element of the design. For them, the completed building is, more or less, a snapshot of the process of intervention. The group's founders, Wolfgang D. Prix and Helmut Swiczinsky, see architecture as both intervention and attack, change and conquest: and in their view this strategy should remain visible. They put these theories into practice at Seibersdorf, creating an imposing new raised block which is set at an angle to the existing structure, rising above the monotony of other institute buildings both literally and metaphorically.

The bare concrete box of the old warehouse was remodelled into a highly flexible public hall. Huge steel girders break through the old building, and the places where it joins with the new construction are exposed as glass-covered fractures. The "de-composed" façade of the office building reveals its layers of blue metal casing, grid screen, and girder bridges, highlighting their various functions: insulation, provision of daylight, protection from the sun, bridge to the world outside. This emphasis on the building's external relief is taken to an extreme in the cube-like retreat which breaks through the surface of the rear façade: a tiny monk's cell dedicated to isolation and reflection.

"In these intersecting, accessible buildings and shapes there are no longer any closed spaces. Only broadly dedicated areas. Areas within the building are no longer contained and defined: they challenge their users to take possession of the space" (Coop Himmelblau). This structural concept based on ideas of openness and autonomy underlies the whole of the institute building (4,300 square metres in all). The architects see in it an analogy with the simultaneity of scientific work. Systems analysts, mathematicians and environmental technologists work in project groups, defined according to the needs of the particular task in hand. The architectural framework offers them adaptibility and flexibility. Partition walls in the offices and in the main hall are made of sliding sections: working areas can be arranged as open spaces or individual units.

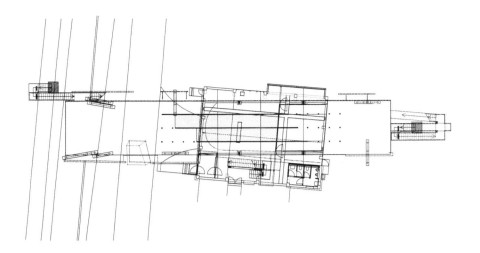

Opposite:

Coop Himmelblau's design is based on the idea of dynamism. Reflecting the varied occupations of its inhabitants, a research group comprising various disciplines, the exterior of the new addition is made up of overlapping yet disparate forms clad in blue sheet metal and glass, articulated further by the occasional use of light-weight mesh panels.

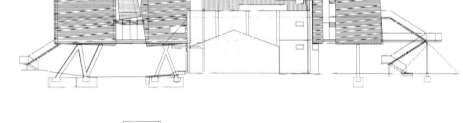

Drawings from top to bottom:

Ground-floor plan.

Elevation and longitudinal sections.

Above left:

The two-storey construction is balanced on sets of spindly legs which straddle a service road.

Above right:

The "monk's cell" breaks through the rear façade – a room dedicated to private thought and relaxation. The exterior panels are built up from inside and contain thermal insulation and a sound-insulating shell.

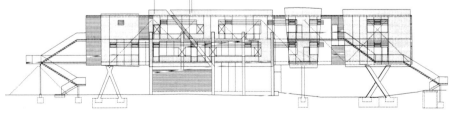

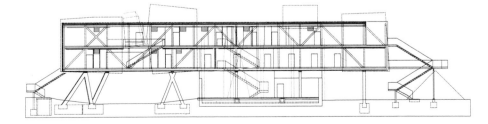

Staircase linking first and second floors.
Office spaces are open but can be
transformed into individual spaces
when required. The movement from one
area to another is kept fluid, with the stair
handrails constructed from wire mesh.

Above left:

The space in the ground-floor auditorium can be subdivided by the use of movable wood and textile walls. Structural elements are in concrete and the walls were built with gypsum board.

Above right:

View up the staircase to the top levels. A potentially dark space has been kept translucent through the use of various forms of glass and perforated metal panels.

4

CYBERTAINMENT

Virtual reality, computer simulations and interactive on-line communication are displaying their crowd-pulling attractions in an abundance of new entertainment and information facilities. Highly equipped games halls have become a testing ground for the latest electronic entertainment technologies – and it is not only telecommunications and media companies who are making use of technology to create attractive "infotainments". Theme restaurants use multimedia props and effects to stage magnificent theatrical spectacles. Internet cafés, targeted at young consumers schooled in the world of computer games, offer a relaxed, practice-orientated entry into the complex on-line consumer worlds that are rapidly evolving. A specialized architectural style is developing in these buildings, where technologies which are essentially geared towards individual use are adapted to suit a public market. Cybertainment finds its architectural counterpart in the stylistic paraphrase of fantasy worlds, science fiction, cartoons and Hollywood style. Whether the result is an over-the-top adventure paradise or an imposing high-tech showroom, in all cases these new collective arenas are used to counteract the fundamental isolation of the computer-screen experience.

PHILIPS FANTASY WORLD, KIRCHHELLEN, GERMANY

ARCHITECT/INTERIOR DESIGNER:
MATTEO THUN
1993

This "fantasy world" presents a fairytale for the electronic age, invented by Italian graphic designer Massimo Giacon: its main characters are the evil dinosaur Rosso and the clever turtle Captain Isy. The story is told through a unique piece of fantasy-architecture: here the world of cartoons becomes a living architectural experience. Generally, theme-park attractions offer second-hand reproductions taken from films, literature or cartoons. The Philips Fantasy World created by Milan-based designer-architect Matteo Thun is the original, presenting its own story and characters.

The fabric-covered metal construction was completed in 1993 as part of the Bavaria Filmpark. The theatre of light which awaits visitors in the depths of its silver dome was produced, along with its soundtrack, by the avant-garde American stage director Robert Wilson. The purpose of the whole project is to popularize and promote new multimedia products. After an introductory display, visitors can use interactive terminals to test the CD-i technology developed by Philips as a bridge between the worlds of television and computers. Dieter Oehms, managing director of Philips Consumer Electronics in Germany, describes the aims of this DM 6 million (£2 million)-project as follows: "Innovative technology must be conveyed through new forms of experiential marketing. Through its multimedia total effect Philips Fantasy World aims to create an exceptional attraction which combines High-Tech, contemporary aesthetics and enjoyment in an intelligent way."

The pavilion, 65 metres long and more than 20 metres high, has its place in a long, romantic tradition of entertainment architecture, which reaches back far beyond the limited illusions of contemporary theme parks to the famous garden follies of the past and the showpiece buildings of the great Universal Expositions. Here a space fantasy is given architectural form, at once expressing a corporate philosophy and making an original contribution to contemporary architecture.

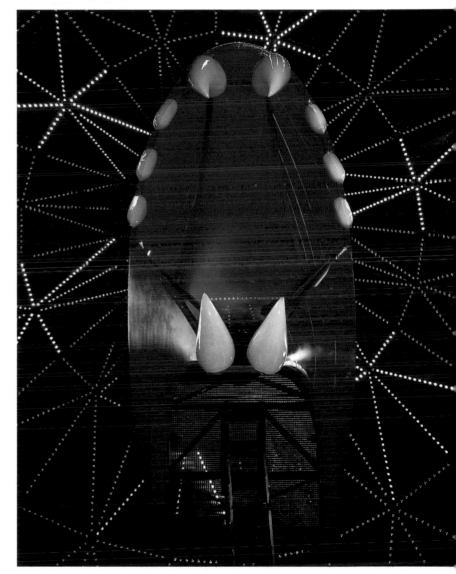

Theatre of light and sound inside the cupola, staged by the American theatre avant-gardist Robert Wilson.

Right and below:

Three sculptural elements form the entertainment complex. Visitors reach the show pavilion through the body of the evil dinosaur, encounter the multi-media devices in the spaceship capsule, and end up in a merchandising shop.

Bottom:

Cross-section of the inclined spaceship.

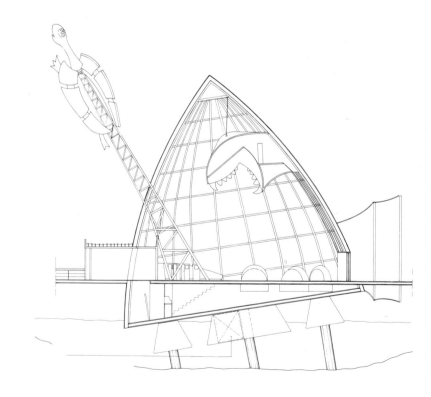

Opposite and below:

**The space capsule rises to over 20m and is surrounded by
two decks of interactive play stations for CD-i software
promoted by Philips.**

PLANET HOLLYWOOD, ORLANDO, USA

ARCHITECT/INTERIOR DESIGNER:
ROCKWELL GROUP
1994

The completion of the Planet Hollywood building in Orlando was a special event even for the hugely successful creators of this fast-growing chain of entertainment restaurants. The new arrival would have to compete against Disney World's powerful attractions so it had to be something special. The building, located right next to Pleasure Island, is a translucent blue globe over 30 metres high, held in place by a support structure of twelve steel buttresses; customers enter through an escalator tube with a UFO disc suspended over it. At night this striking apparition is covered with shimmering coloured lights and looks as if it has just landed on earth.

The Rockwell Group has been responsible for the "Planet Hollywood" designs for several years now, with more than thirty outlets to its credit. For this building it inflated the company logo into a huge architectural fantasy. Even the inside of the magic ball takes the traditional stage-effects based on props and images from America's dream-factory into new dimensions. Above the different restaurant areas hang eleven tonnes of Hollywood memorabilia, ranging from a jet cockpit to costumed figurines and a VW-Beetle. A big alligator slowly winds along a circular path over the customers' heads. A huge screen and countless monitors show compilations of classic film scenes, popular music videos and film preview clips. The panoramic theatrical interior displays the great stars and settings of cinema history, highlighted by ingenious lighting effects.

The concept of theme restaurants is not a new one in itself: but projects like the one in Orlando give it a new dimension, creating a leisure category of their own. The restaurant itself takes a back seat to the three-dimensional spectacle, in which setting and props have assumed the leading roles. The customers are there firstly for the visual experience: the meal is secondary to the show. The next stage is already under way: the Rockwell Group is currently developing preliminary studies for interactive adventure-cafés, where virtual 3-D encounters with superheroes like Spiderman or Captain America are served up with a hamburger and Coke.

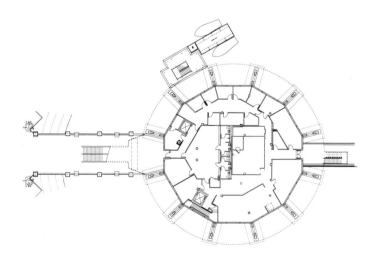

Opposite top:

Entrance to the main dining area is through a semicircular gilded arch.

Below:

The Planet Hollywood in Walt Disney World follows over thirty designs for the restaurant chain executed by the Rockwell Group. The free-standing structure is located next to Pleasure Island and composed as a giant three-dimensional version of the company's logo. Rising to more than 30m, the translucent blue globe is accessed via an illuminated escalator.

Drawings from left:

Main dining room, lower and upper mezzanine floor plans.

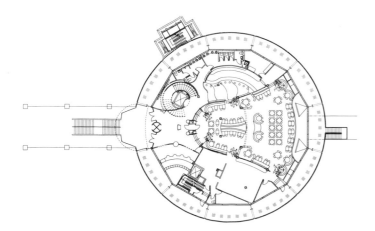 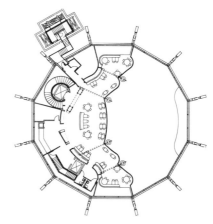

Views down from the second mezzanine and across the ground-floor restaurant. The interior is futuristic, yet at the same time reminiscent of the baroque interiors of music-hall theatres, with their over-decoration and tiered balconies. The space which pushes through three floors contains the largest diorama in the world, which curves around the interior surfaces of the walls.

CAFÉ CYBERIA,
PARIS, FRANCE

INTERIOR DESIGNER:
BERNHARD BLAUEL ARCHITECTS
1995

The Pompidou Centre was way ahead of all other arts institutions when it staged its pioneering exhibition "Les Immatériaux" in the early 1980s, examining the theoretical, philosophical and creative outlook for virtual technologies. The subject only became popular once multimedia and the Internet had begun to develop into communications technologies for the masses. Now the arts factory of Paris is again at the cutting edge: over the central ticketing area it has installed one of the computer-cafés which are becoming popular with young Net surfers. The icon of the architectural avant-garde (built in 1975–76) is beginning to feel its age and is undergoing a general renovation: the new Café Cyberia makes a small but significant contribution to redefining its function and aims.

The successful British operating company already has a number of Internet cafés trading under the same name; it commissioned architect Bernhard Blauel, who works in London, to design the branch in the French capital as a prototype for new outlets planned for the future. Blauel was given a tiny budget of only £58,000 to deal with the huge challenge posed by this eminent location: nonetheless he succeeded in creating a functional and aesthetically satisfying solution. He used plywood walls and screens of wire mesh to define the shape of the mezzanine gallery; the café area itself covers 120 square metres. The cables of the 18 computer terminals are channelled through the "light beam", a large, back-lit fixture which runs the full length of the ceiling.

All components of the construction were pre-assembled; the work took only eight weeks to complete, including installation on site. "Minimum intervention to achieve maximum effect", was the architect's declared aim; "to build a frame around an activity, to reduce materiality to a minimum, to use industrial, rough materials and finishes, to deal with a possible maximum of 1,200 people a day" (Blauel).

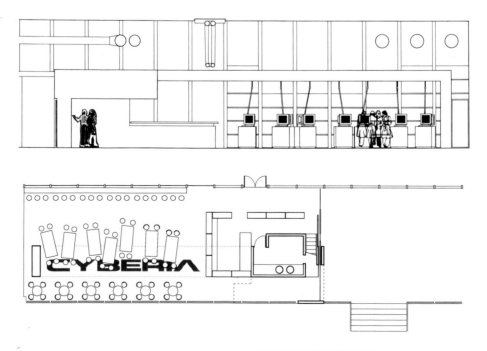

Floor plan and cross-section.

Below left:
Mesh screens are used instead of balustrades,
allowing views into the main space of the
ground floor of the Pompidou Centre.

Below right:
Situated on the upper mezzanine level of the
Pompidou Centre in Paris, the Café Cyberia marks
the arrival of multimedia in this great realm of
the arts.

All computer desks are connected by
means of flexible conduits to a central
beam which spans the café area.
Blauel has used industrial materials
and rough finishes. The bar counter
has a welded galvanized steel frame
with chipboard front panels clad with
"Nomad" cushion plus matting.

OZ CITY, TOKYO, JAPAN

ARCHITECT/INTERIOR DESIGNER:
C&A ARCHITECTS
1995

In recent years a new electronic entertainment quarter has grown up in Tokyo's shopping district of Shibuya. "Digital Nightclubbing" is all the rage here, with TV-discos, computer cafés and virtual games halls. The most comprehensive range of services for cyber-yuppies can be found in Oz City. This stylish, free-standing corner building with a transparent metal mesh wall surrounding the roof offers entertainment, infotainment and business on six storeys. The ground floor and mezzanine are reserved for a more traditional type of business, with the high-class décor of Escot's Grill. However, from the second floor upwards the media age holds sway.

The second-floor bar is called DUG, and it promises a "digital underground", and "luxury for liberal adults": customers at this establishment can recline on soft cushions, while surfing gently through the Internet or special software on a laptop. The bar is also equipped for live multimedia events transmitted by means of television or data networks.

On the third floor of the building is Oz City Travel, an ultra-modern travel agent: clients can plan their holidays electronically, using computers to check prices, to play videos of their travel destinations and to make their booking. The floor above this is a paradise for the joystick fraternity, with densely packed rows of games machines. On the top floor we return to a calmer ambience: the Cyber Net Café offers the usual combination of refreshments and World Wide Web. The equipment and software available here is always right up to the minute: manufacturers are keen to present their latest products to their target consumer market.

Oz City's mix of leisure and shopping, information and business, points the way to future developments in the retail and catering sectors. This multifunctional project is also exemplary in stylistic terms. It does not flog the usual cheap fairground effects but maintains a consistently high level of design quality: cybernauts are moving upmarket.

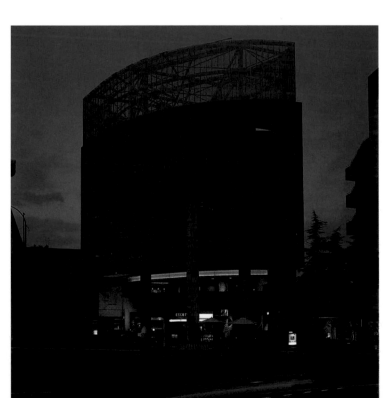

Left:
The building is a multifunctional wired hotspot for dining, net-surfing and entertainment.

Opposite:
Connecting stairway in the stylish Escot's Grill restaurant.

Below:

Floor plans. The ground floor and mezzanine are reserved for restaurant facilities; the second floor has a digital bar, the third is an ultramodern travel agency; the fourth is a games arcade; and the fifth a cyber café.

Opposite:

The sleek use of polished wood and the minimalist interior of the cyber café (*bottom*) is in direct contrast to the DUG bar (*top*) which is described as "luxury for liberal adults". Here, customers can sit on brightly covered soft chairs, take a drink and surf the Internet on a laptop. Alternatively, through Cyber Diver software, they can enjoy virtual galleries containing the work of contemporary artists.

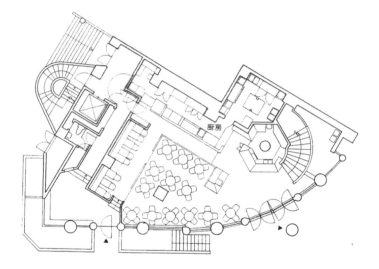

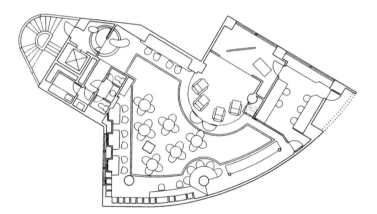

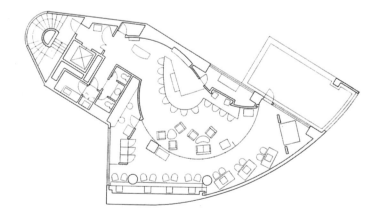

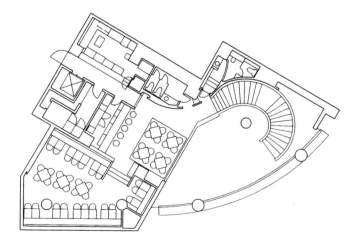

INFO BOX,
BERLIN, GERMANY

ARCHITECT:
SCHNEIDER + SCHUMACHER
INTERIOR DESIGNER:
D & D KOMMUNIKATIONSDESIGN
1995

Forty years of division have left their mark on the city of Berlin – and nowhere has history inflicted deeper scars than on the Potsdamer Platz. This city-centre site is now a focal point for new development projects, financed by powerful investors. This is not simply a question of one or two mega-projects: a whole new urban landscape will have been conjured out of nothing by the end of the millennium. Marketing and promotional efforts for the redevelopment scheme were started at an early stage, with the aim of creating widespread acceptance and high levels of awareness among the public.

An information pavilion, a central element of the campaign, was the first building to be completed in this urban wasteland. As befits the setting and the occasion this is not just an ordinary functional construction but a bright red box of metal and glass set on high stilts, a signpost pointing to Berlin's future. The building, called the Info Box, has proved an architectural hit. The Frankfurt architects Till Schneider and Michael Schumacher consciously adopted an industrial style of design. Their huge container, a 60-metre-long pre-fabricated unit of concrete and steel, was mounted on the eight-metre-high support structure on site; the project took only three months to complete. The building has simple metal stairways on the exterior and interior; its open and flexible design includes an auditorium, a café and a shop. Each of the companies involved in developing the Potsdamer

Heralding the new and discarding the past. As the old Berlin wall is demolished, Schneider and Schumacher's shiny steel-concrete container at the Potsdamer Platz houses the information centre of the most important developers.

Platz was allocated an area of 1,000 square metres where it could give an in-depth multimedia presentation of its technological and architectural plans. The "infotainment" is pepped up by interactive electronics, turning the Info Box into a dazzling televisual experience. Large-screen simulations allow visitors to fly over the new quarters of the city, computer animation enables them to experience futuristic forms of transport, touch-screens turn them into virtual architects and transport them into a new consumer age.

The project set ambitious goals, seeking to turn this huge building site into a tourist attraction and bolster its image. It has been an overwhelming success. The Info Box, which cost DM 20 million (£8.25 million), has become Berlin's leading public attraction, with more than one million visitors per year. The crowds will disperse after New Year's Eve, 2000: by that time the red box of tricks and visions will have served its purpose, and must make way for the real buildings of the new Berlin.

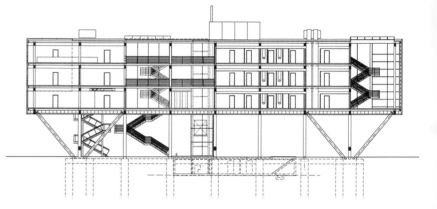

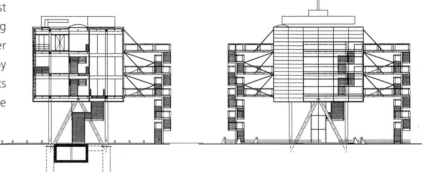

Front and side elevations. The box has three floors and two divisions. The side facing Potsdamer Platz houses a shopping area on the first floor, a communal space on the second and a café on the third. Here building progress can be monitored over a cup of tea. The other side consists solely of exhibition areas. The whole is surmounted by a rooftop terrace with panoramic views over the surrounding cityscape.

Opposite:
Schneider and Schumacher's bright red pavilion is constructed of metal and glass and is set high on stilts.

CYBERSMITH,
WHITE PLAINS, USA

INTERIOR DESIGNER:
FITCH
1996

American entrepreneur Marshall Smith has made his fortune by identifying new consumer markets at an early stage and developing innovative retail concepts to exploit their potential. His retail chains Paperback Booksmith, Videosmith and Learningsmith are well-established in the shopping malls of the United States. Now Smith is looking to break into the on-line multimedia sector with Cybersmith, a carefully crafted combination of Internet café and software retailer. The marketing concept was based on the observation that Internet enthusiasts stayed for hours surfing the World Wide Web in low-profile specialist outlets, where they spent little on food and drink: here was a market with clear potential for generating much higher revenues.

The new retail format gives consumers the opportunity to experiment with new technologies, offering them a mixture of effort-free learning and "infotainment", of interactive enjoyment and shopping. Its aim is to attract a broader public to the world of virtual consumerism: the market of the future.

The design commission for Cybersmith went to the London consultancy Fitch, internationally recognized specialists in marketing and brand development. In collaboration with Boston architects Schwartz Silver they came up with a turnkey design system for Cybersmith branches. After a pilot project in Cambridge, Massachusetts, the first outlet in White Plains, New York marks the beginning of a nation-wide programme of branch openings. "The future of retail will depend on restructuring the rules to make money by selling time within environments": this is how Fitch director Neil Whitehead describes his aim. In consequence, visitors to Cybersmith are first and foremost users rather than purchasers or customers. They use a chip card to pay for access to the Apple terminals and the 3-D computer games; their Internet units are charged by the minute. Users who decide to buy the latest CD-ROMs get a refund on their testing time. In this virtual world you can get real food and drink at reasonable prices: you can order a cappuccino or a sandwich from the on-screen menu with a click of the mouse.

Left:
Floor plan.

Opposite top:
The mix of software, retail and multimedia café forms the new marketing concept.

Opposite bottom:
Booths can seat up to three people and contain Apple computers.

The design of Cybersmith is targeted in terms of a series of franchise facilities all over the USA. The essence is to create an ambience to explore new software and surf the net.

TELECOM WORLD, HONG KONG

INTERIOR DESIGNER:
MET STUDIO
1995

"A compelling experience in sight, sound and touch, a fascinating voyage of discovery in the extraordinary world of telecommunications": this is what the Hong Kong subsidiary of British company Cable & Wireless promises visitors to its new attraction Telecom World. The London design agency MET Studio converted 4,300 square metres of Telecom Tower into a multimedia promotional paradise, with a budget of HK $100 million (£8.33 million). The delights of computer-based information and entertainment products are presented in a series of seven educational displays with over one hundred pieces of equipment for visitors to use. Entrance is free of charge: the company is looking to attract school groups in particular.

Telecom World is a candid demonstration of how marketing strategists in the new information age can gain easy access to tomorrow's unsuspecting consumers: every visitor is given a personalized smart card as their plastic key to this virtual paradise. Of course, this does more than just activate the "infotainment" machines; it is also a highly effective market-research tool, storing each user's preferences and habits. The double-edged quality of these methods, combining entertainment and observation, provides much food for thought, especially in the context of Hong Kong, which is soon to fall under China's Communist rule. Yet in architectural terms Telecom World is flawless, setting new stylistic and technological standards for architects of information and entertainment facilities. Visitors are taken on a journey through time, from the very beginnings of telecommunication, right up to the threshold of tomorrow's world: "Just Imagine" is the title of the final chamber of delights. Smart displays present simulations of flight situations and medical operations, data files and human figures appear on the "living office wall" at the push of a button, an electronic butler at home follows digital instructions to the letter. This is a "soft sell", to use the corporate catchword, but the underlying message is clear: telecommunications is presented as the key to a utopian future.

Above:

Reception area: in order to create an illusion of space in what is essentially an office area, MET have designed double-height areas at certain points. In the foreground there is a "smart-card" terminal. On entry, the visitor keys in details of age, language preferences, level of understanding and any special interests, and receives a card. The card is then used in special information stands and ensures that the journey of discovery is adapted to the needs of the individual.

Opposite top:

The exhibition is divided into seven themed areas. These are decorated in warm colours, using natural materials in the rooms dealing with the history of telecommunications, and in space-age tones of blue and silver lit by neon when exploring telecommunications of the future.

Opposite bottom:

"Getting connected" has several experiments and demonstrations on the "school boy principle" of a length of string and two cans.

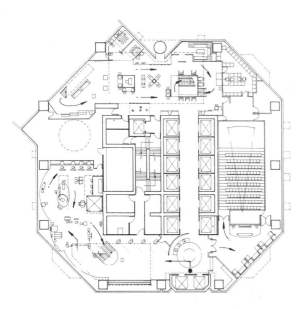

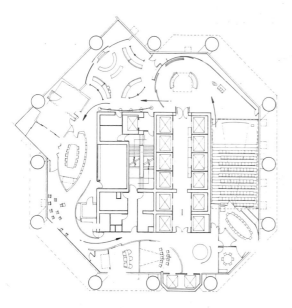

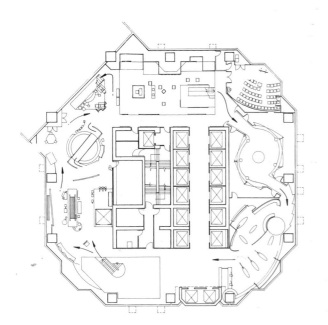

Floor plans:

Telecom World is a business showcase as well as an exhibition. With over 100 interactive exhibits in seven galleries, occupying 4,300 square metres on two floors, it is situated in Hong Kong Telecom's headquarters and has become part of their corporate identity. A third floor has a 100-seat auditorium, and video-conferencing rooms and business suites.

Right:

The "Just Imagine" gallery is at the end of the exploration of telecommunication, and looks at future technological developments. Here the interaction between the human and modern technology is most evident. In an atmosphere of constantly changing light and sound, visitors place their hands into conical towers to activate talking heads which appear in irregular apertures in the walls of the structure.

FUTUREVISION, MANCHESTER, UK

INTERIOR DESIGNER:
JOHN CSÀKY/BUTTON COMMUNICATIONS GROUP
1996

Coronation Street and cyberspace are now only a few feet apart. The latest attraction in the Granada television company's Manchester theme park is designed to transport its visitors into the fast-approaching future of television. "Futurevision" was opened in May 1996: this "infotainment" centre operated by Granada Studio Tours cost £1 million and covers an area of 1,050 square metres. It is divided into seven sections, presenting a multimedia demonstration of how progress in communications technology will alter our lives. "At the concept stage we identified that Granada needed some kind of educational attraction to complement what was already there, but it needed to appeal to people who knew nothing about the subjects", explains architect John Csaky from the London design group Button Communications, which supervised the project.

Futurevision is designed as a tour, but it does not impose a rigid time-frame on its visitors, who can follow their interests and stay as long as they like at the different interactive stations. This journey into the media world of the future begins with an exploration of the history of television and the current state of the medium. The next section whets visitors' appetites for the new digital pay-TV channels which have already started to invade the home. The following sections transport visitors into the World Wide Web of the Internet (under an eight-metre dome) and demonstrate the changing nature of office work (with data-transfer and video-conferencing technologies). After this, visitors can sample the delights of teleshopping, and the tour ends in the futuristic comfort of a fully computerized high-tech home.

With the exception of a few striking techno-effect settings, Futurevision uses an astonishingly restrained design vocabulary and top-class graphic design. The intention is to convey the fascination of the new media world through the electronic technology itself and not through extravagant showbiz-style trappings. The public response will show whether this austere approach is the best way to educate the masses.

Opposite:

A 12-metre-high mast houses ten live television screens and ascends through the lobby and main exhibition space.

Below:

The 7-metre-high translucent dome contains the "Onto the Web" exhibit which explores cyberspace.

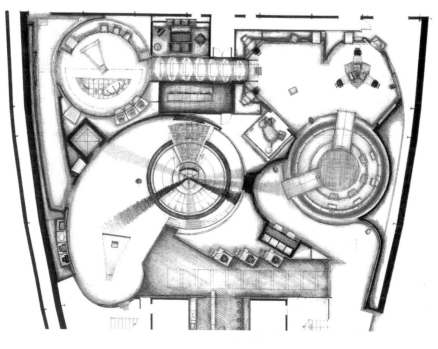

Opposite top and above:

The different galleries incorporate a vast array of state-of-the-art computers, television and high-tech equipment, demonstrating how technology will change the way we live. The designers have used a restrained design vocabulary without excessive gimmickry, allowing the technology to speak for itself in direct interaction with the visitor.

Below:

The floor plan (*opposite*) and elevation (*right*) show the positioning of the seven themed areas within the 1,050-square-metre space at Granada Studios.

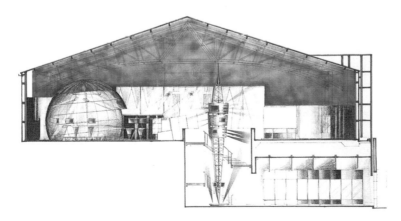

VIRTUAL WORLD CENTER, PASADENA, USA

INTERIOR DESIGNER:
PICA & SULLIVAN ARCHITECTS
1994

It must be in the family genes: somehow the name Disney is always connected with entertainment products which are virtually unrivalled for quality, poise and user-friendliness. When Tim Disney, grand-nephew of the legendary Walt, decided to set himself up in the new sector of interactive computer games, he wanted to turn the cheap fun arcades full of electronic battle-tech into professionally designed, stimulating adventure scenarios. Disney developed his digital theme park concept in collaboration with architects Pica & Sullivan. A chain of these theme parks is planned, trading under the brand name Virtual World: more than twenty branches have already been opened in the USA, Canada, Japan and the United Kingdom.

These are no ordinary penny arcades. Virtual World (which has a floor space of 700 square metres in Pasadena) tells an exciting story and leads its visitors into a futuristic fantasy world. The fiction begins right at the entrance: visitors are received in the Jules Verne-style interior of a Victorian scientists' club – because the Virtual World is an outlet of the secret society Virtual Geographic League. In the Explorers' Lounge, with its bar and library, visitors pre-pare for their virtual adventures through space and time. As the launching time approaches, up to eight expedition members enter Containment Bay, a cross between NASA Control and Edison's garage workshop, fitted out with all the technical props. Here they receive their instructions and watch a short introductory film, choose their code name and enter the simulation cabins which are packed with monitors (the usual VR-headsets are not needed here). Ten minutes later, when the chases through mineshafts on Mars and the robot battles on hostile planets are over, the players can relive their adventures, victories and defeats on video. They all receive a computer printout as a souvenir of their virtual mission.

The architects define their off-the-peg adventureland as "an environment which tells the story to the patron by the architecture – not by the spoken word. The Virtual World Center is a three-act play." Real props and historical stage settings compensate for the unreality of digital simulation: this ingenious device is the secret of success. Even the books on the library shelves are real: the designers stipulated only that the word adventure should appear in every title.

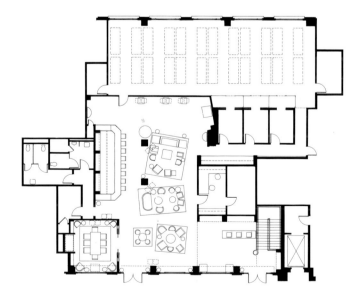

Opposite:

To make the most of the limited floor space available, Joseph Pica has kept to a simple design which follows the progress of the visitor's journey through reception, departure zone, to the briefing room and finally into the containment bay. There is a also a centrally placed lounge and bar.

Right:

The Virtual World equivalent of H. G. Wells' *Time Machine* is situated intrusively in the lounge area, a club member's "work in progress". Inside can be glimpsed the computers necessary to transport the traveller to another dimension.

Below right:

The Explorers' Lounge is an eclectic mixture of styles and meant to refer to the London-based Geographic Society of the 1900s. Once there the visitor takes on the identity of a great explorer waiting to travel to, or talking about his voyages of discovery into, the twenty-first century.

Opposite:

The transition from the Edwardian interior of the lounge to the futuristic briefing area is through a corridor lined with chemistry sets, mainframe computers and pilot lockers.

Right:

The Virtual World pods are located in the containment bay. Here the latest in technology is surrounded by an unsophisticated industrial design, with the high-tech wiring and ventilation needed to run the machines situated in conduits running unapologetically across the ceiling and directly into the stations.

Below right:

The detail of a banister has a nautical theme taken, no doubt, from Jules Verne's *Twenty Thousand Leagues under the Sea.*

THE TROCADERO, SEGAWORLD, LONDON, UK

ARCHITECTS:
RTKL UK LTD, TIBBATTS ASSOCIATES
1996

Segaworld is housed in London's Piccadilly Circus on the top floors of the Trocadero, which has been transformed by RTKL UK Ltd, the international architectural design and planning firm, into a futuristic pleasure dome and pre-eminent urban leisure complex. Visitors are conveyed as make-believe space travellers from this world to Segaworld on the Launch and Rocket escalators lit with flickering neon and laser beams. On the way they pass "The Show", a multimedia extravaganza played out on a wall of more than 100 video monitors and on two giganitc pillars which rise through the full height of the scheme. "For the Trocadero we scripted a storyboard of 'events' that we wanted visitors or shoppers to experience as they circulated through the building. This experience reaches a climax with Segaworld", comments RTKL.

The Japanese manufacturer Sega is synonymous with its computer games, which have revolutionized the youth culture of today. For children and young people throughout the world these virtual adventures at the end of a joystick have become a favourite leisure pursuit. However, this superpower of computerized entertainment, the creator of bestsellers such as "Super Sonic", "Mortal Combat" and "Dune II", is not resting on its laurels. Sega is already pursuing its next conquest: a global network of entertainment centres which are designed to transform the computer-game experience into an interactive cyberspace adventure. Segaworld is the first of these lavish indoor theme parks, described by Sega in the following terms: "In contrast to the attractions of the past which could only be experienced by passive viewing, visitors can create their own view of the world through active participation, enjoying the freedom of shaping the encounter at will".

Tibbatts Associates, design consultants and architects, have created an electronic wonderland on six levels with a total floor space of 11,840 square metres. Visitors are sent on specially designed escalators to the top floor where the first attraction awaits them, and the downward journey is packed with electronic entertainment, passing through six adventure areas, including among others the Combat Zone, the Race Track and the Sports Arena. A genuine RAF Harrier jump jet hovers over the Flight Deck. The large-scale interactive installations are especially impressive, including 3-D ghost trains complete with movement, wind and noise effects, and Aqua Planet, where combat cars engage in furious running battles. Wearing VR-headsets or in flight simulators, visitors can glide through the far reaches of space repelling interstellar attacks. Most of the displays follow the familiar formula of Sega's computer games: the player's skill and number of hits decide the course and outcome of the game. Even here, though, the basic dilemma of electronic simulations cannot be resolved altogether by the transformation into total experience: the computerized illusion can only be perfect if the individual's field of perception is narrowed down as far as possible. The deciding factor is the illusion-creating machinery; its setting is relatively unimportant. Whatever the futuristic backdrop, the real Sega experience takes place in the visitor's head, equipped for the purpose with a pair of cyber-goggles (a 650-gramme head-mounted display).

Neon-lit futurist escalators transport cybernauts from street level to the top floor of the Trocadero's Segaworld, passing giant screen walls with the latest virtual entertainment news.

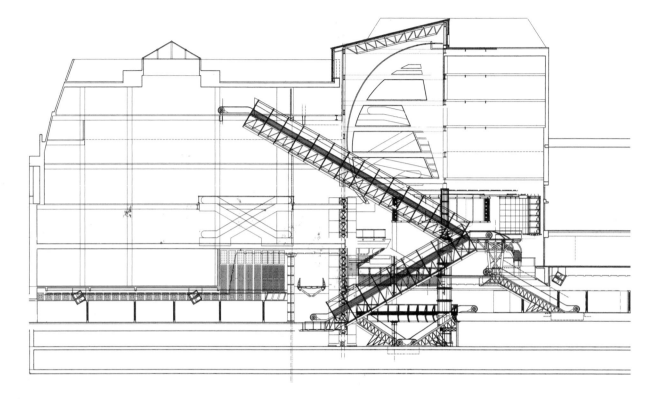

Opposite top:

Opposite top:

Section of the Trocadero remodelling. The landmark complex near London's Piccadilly Circus was completely shied open to make room for the Segaworld scheme.

Opposite bottom:

To experience the intergalactic adventures, visitors have to board shiny spaceship pods which are fully equipped simulators that use the latest VR technologies.

Above:

The Flight Deck dominated by a real Harrier jump jet is just one of the themed zones offering interactive play stations and sight and sound experiences.

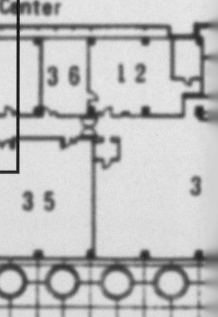

5

KNOWLEDGE EXCHANGES

The digital revolution has finally begun to conquer the realms of academia and the intellect. The delay can be explained by the habitual tightness of public finances, and also by an inherent resistance to change on the part of the cultural and educational institutions themselves. Traditional storage and information media like the book and periodical are being supplemented by the new electronic data products and network services. What was once the province of student Internet-fanatics is now becoming a standard feature of academic life. Catalogue searches and scientific investigations are undertaken on screen; specialist periodicals and publications can be accessed by computer; databases, archives and research information are searched on-line. The invasion of electronic media is changing the appearance and functions of libraries, institutes and cultural centres. Not by replacing their traditional programme of functions: it is simply being redefined in a contemporary way. This can be seen most clearly in the renaissance of libraries. Today, the educational temple of the last century is metamorphosing into a digitally-networked knowledge exchange. For all these functional changes no radical modification of architectural style is necessary: the traditional combination of solemnity and improvised workshop style prevails.

MAIN PUBLIC LIBRARY, SAN FRANCISCO, USA

ARCHITECT/INTERIOR DESIGNER:
PEI COBB FREED & PARTNERS
1996

The library's opening date was not intended as a bad omen: the dazzling white granite building on City Hall Plaza opened its doors ninety years to the day after the great San Francisco earthquake. A single glance is enough to receive convincing evidence of the seismic stability of this massive structure, which reflects the diversity of its setting, with four different façade fronts. However, its architecture is not so persuasive, unless we are to see a new "American Style" in this mixture of crude historicism and recycled Art Deco, combined with touches of ultra-modern "de-composition" and professional shopping-mall chic. The design by James Ingo Freed tries to achieve too much at once. Firstly, it seeks to form a counterpart to the beaux-arts ensemble of the San Francisco Civic Center. Secondly, it tries to bridge the gap between these public buildings and the financial centre of the Californian metropolis. Thirdly, it aims to modernize its genre: in Freed's words, "This building brings the library fully into the twenty-first century".

Works of art commissioned from such respected contemporary stars as Alice Aycock contribute involuntarily to the ambivalence of the overall design, which obscures the undoubted quality of the building's internal organization. Inside, on a floor space of nearly 40,500 square metres, the traditional library format, with its limited cultural function of displaying and storing books, is reinterpreted in a thoroughly contemporary way. The central atrium and numerous smaller courtyards bring ample natural light into the public areas and reading rooms of the six-storey building, creating varied and atmospheric interior spaces. Here, on the threshold of Silicon Valley, it was not difficult to achieve the architect's third aim: his granite marvel bristles with high-tech electronic equipment. Reading desks are equipped with cable wells and laptop sockets. There are more than 300 workstations where readers can browse through catalogues, periodicals and databases, or even surf the Internet. A dozen high-performance multimedia computers and video-conference rooms complete the impressive range of interactive facilities on offer.

San Francisco's characteristic emphasis on multiculturalism and socio-cultural minorities is reflected in a multitude of specialist departments, each with its own multimedia information facilities and services: these include the African-American Center, the Chinese Center, the Filipino-American Center, a Latino Focus Collection, and Environmental Center, as well as the Children's Electronic Discovery Center and the Gay and Lesbians Center. The library also has a video library for the deaf and speaking terminals for the blind. Despite its rather ponderous architecture this makes a lively and likeable arts centre, fully in tune with the needs of its community.

The new Main Library completes the beaux-arts ensemble of San Francisco's Civic Center.

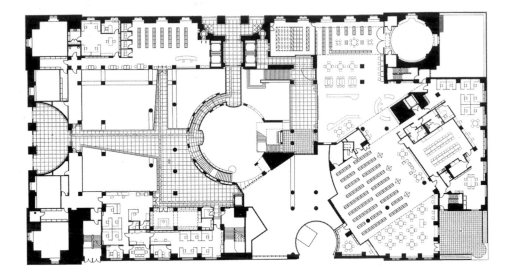

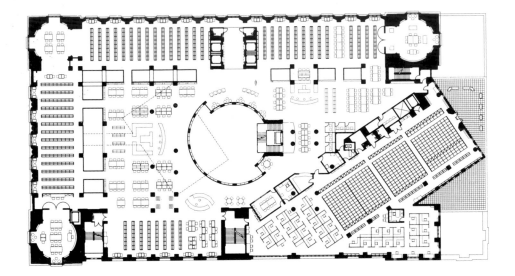

Drawings from top:

Upper main and second-floor plans. The architect has created a play between volume and space. A top-lit atrium, internal courtyards and connecting walkways between functional areas all help to flood the colossal building with light.

Section. The glazed central atrium is enclosed by two six-storey wings. Freed conceived of a building that would combine a working library with a civic meeting-place and has created contiguous voids which act as an interior urban public space.

Opposite:

The skylight is not symmetrical but slightly askew and is made from clear and translucent glass which casts patterns of rotating light. The main staircase juts out into the atrium, giving views from the upper floors, as does the wedge-shaped glazed periodical reading room which rises through the skylight to maximize natural illumination.

The internal organization of spaces in the
reading areas is thoroughly contemporary and
contrasts sharply with the historicist outer shell.

One of eight Special Collection rooms distinguished
from the rest of the building by their warm palette
and custom-designed metalwork in a sort of Art
Deco revival. The walls use maple-wood panels,
as does the ceiling but with the addition of a stainless-steel floating disc with built-in custom lighting.

MEDIA PARK,
ICHIKAWA, JAPAN

ARCHITECT/INTERIOR DESIGNER:
YAMASHITA SEKKEI
1994

Even municipal cultural centres have not escaped the multimedia revolution: the town of Ichikawa in the prefecture of Chiba chose the name "Media Park" for its new educational complex. This 175-metre-long brick building (with a floor space of nearly 20,000 square metres) combines traditional and progressive services in a sensible and accessible way. The town's governors wanted "a citizens' forum, which can be utilized by all citizens, from children to senior citizens, as their base for lifelong learning". The project was to unite four institutions under one roof: the Municipal Central Library, a Central Children's Pavilion, the Visual Culture Centre and the local Education Centre.

Architects Yamashita Sekkei opted for a single large building which is divided internally, presenting a clear contrast to its disparate setting in terms both of material and structure. The urban qualities of the setting are internalized: the architectural landscape of the Media Park features an abundance of internal open spaces, including terraces, open-air staircases, courtyards and a water-garden surrounded by glass walls next to the main entrance. The four divisions of this cultural centre operate independently of one another and their different functions are concentrated in separate areas. The entrance foyer on the ground floor leads to the Children's Pavilion (on two levels at one end of the building) and the library, which takes up the remainder of this storey. Lifts and staircases lead to the two upper storeys. The Visual Culture Centre is on the first floor; its events hall is also served by a separate entrance on the terrace. The top storey houses the Education Centre's seminar and computer rooms.

The building aims to reach a broad public, using both classic educational means and the new media: this balance is reflected in the restrained stylistic language of the architecture, which does not seek to impress with high-tech decor but focuses on the essential forms and content of this citizens' forum. The same is true of the interior decoration, down to the smallest details. Lighting is used to enhance the architectural effects. Library readers sit in open areas divided only by mid-height bookshelves. Computer users on the floor above work in study cells covered by metal canopies. And in the children's area, alongside the futuristic play tunnel and modern educational software, there is also a small oasis of calm in the room reserved for storytelling.

Above:

Media Park is located on a 19,647-square-metre site in the centre of Ichikawa and consists of the Municipal Library, Central Children's Pavilion, Cultural Centre and Education Facility. The centre has been faced with brick. This is unusual for Japan as bricks have a poor resistance to earthquakes. Yamashita Sekkei, however, have persevered in finding a technology to solve this problem and have thus created a unique landmark.

Opposite:

The main library (*below*) runs north to south on the first floor and is overlooked by an open corridor in the Visual Image Culture Centre above. There video booths are placed in a strip formation (*top*), each marked by a beacon of light which is projected up on to the ceiling, mimicking the lights of the library. Here, top-lit pavilions, which form a decorative detail on the façade, send diffused natural light through circular sandblasted glass panels.

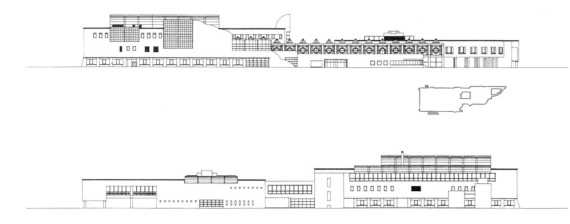

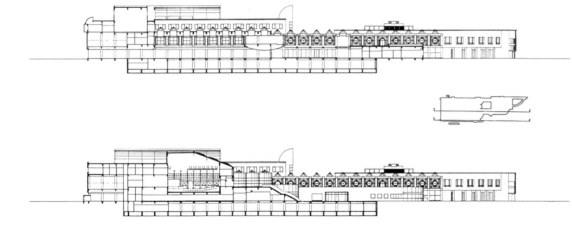

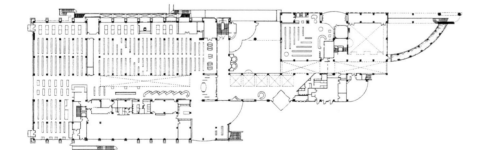

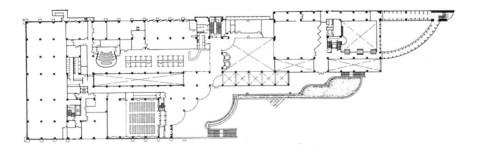

Drawings from top:
East and west elevations and sections.
First- and second-floor plans.

Opposite top:
The Water Plaza is situated directly opposite the entrance plaza. Verticality is emphasized by the addition of two strip elevators and a 17-metre-high sculpture.

Opposite bottom:
The auditorium serves for film and video presentations.

LAW FACULTY, CAMBRIDGE, UK

ARCHITECT:
SIR NORMAN FOSTER AND PARTNERS
1995

The site in Cambridge, right next to James Stirling's momentous History Faculty building of 1968, presented Sir Norman Foster with a particular challenge. His design for the new Law Faculty won a restricted competition because he was the only entrant to take the context into account, integrating his striking, partly transparent, semi-cylindrical building almost organically with the existing architectural fabric of the site. This new university building, which was completed in 1995, radiates both respectfulness and self-confidence. It illustrates a continuing shift in the architect's style, towards large geometrical forms: in contrast to Foster's other library projects of recent years (in Cranfield, United Kingdom and Nîmes, France), in this case he does not make use of an oversized roof structure which overshadows the building itself. Nonetheless even in Cambridge the overall effect, on the interior and the exterior, is dominated by the splendid roof, which arches up from ground level, reaching well above the level of the ridge.

In order to provide the required 9,000 square metres of usable floor space, the building has to delve two storeys below ground level. The lecture halls and seminar rooms are located in these basement levels. The administrative offices are housed on the ground floor and the library occupies the three upper storeys, which are suspended freely in the reclining glass cylinder. Reading desks are arranged in the glass front (made of triangular sections), while the bookshelves are located in the closed, vertical side of the building to the south. For all the modernism of the architectural style, the library area is designed in a sober, traditional manner. This suits the conservative character of the legal profession (although progressive lawyers have long made use of on-line databases and electronic catalogues). Nevertheless, the building is amply provided with progressive technologies: the facilities are managed without the use of air conditioning (except in the basement levels), and an energy-saving lighting-control system regulates the balance between natural and artificial light.

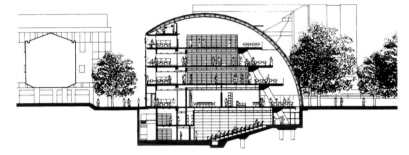

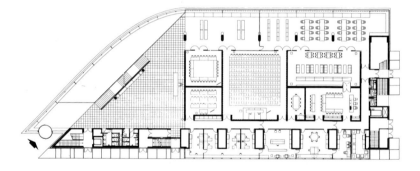

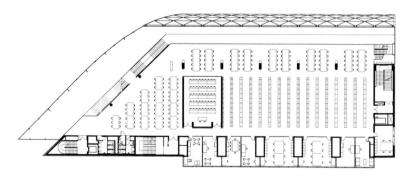

Drawings from top:

Elevation. The three top floors are devoted to the library. Stacks, offices and services are placed along the back wall, while readers' tables face the curved glass façade. The basement is used for lecture halls.

First-floor plan

Second-floor plan

Below:

The fully glazed north elevation of the Cambridge Law Faculty allows light to penetrate deep into the building and also affords generous views out on to the lawns and mature trees of its site.

The three concrete floors of the library are raked and overlook the atrium which rises through the height of the building, creating a lofty spaciousness.

West elevation with view into the main body of the library

BIBLIOTHÈQUE NATIONALE DE FRANCE, PARIS, FRANCE

ARCHITECT:
DOMINIQUE PERRAULT
1995–97

The late French President, François Mitterrand, decided on both the architect and the completion date for the new National Library, the last of his "grands projets" in Paris: he chose the youngest entrant in the competition, and scheduled the completion of this valedictory monument for the end of his period of office in 1995. The resistance to Mitterrand's first monumental project, I.M. Pei's glass pyramid in the forecourt of the Louvre, was a mere whisper in comparison with the storm of public indignation which erupted when Dominique Perrault was announced as the winner. Perrault promised "a square for Paris, a library for France", but nobody seemed to want his hyperminimalist creation, two-thirds concealed by a wooden platform and framed by four glass tower blocks at the corners. However, since it has been completed and can be seen at close quarters, the newest monument in the French capital is gradually winning the approval that it surely deserves. This symbolic building (which cost FF 7.8 billion – nearly £1 billion) effectively conveys the message Mitterrand wanted to put across: "France should make clear, in the form of an exemplary monument, both her sense of the value of her intellectual heritage and her confidence in the future of books and the act of reading".

This is the largest new library building in the world and its dimensions are colossal: the extended complex stands on a plot measuring 7.5 hectares; it has 168,000 square metres of usable floor space and can hold 12 million books. These are stored in the four glass towers (each nearly 80 metres high) and in sections of the building's six-storey base, which houses the library itself. There are separate reading-rooms for academics and the general public, with over 3,500 seats, arranged around an internal courtyard planted with trees. This miniature forest turns nature into a living metaphor, set at the heart of the building's geometrical landscape.

When the library is officially opened in 1997, its users will have the latest electronic technology at their disposal. Books are transported on a computer-controlled track network, and are delivered to the reader twenty minutes after they have been ordered. Library users can access the general catalogue and specialist bibliographies on-line, even from their

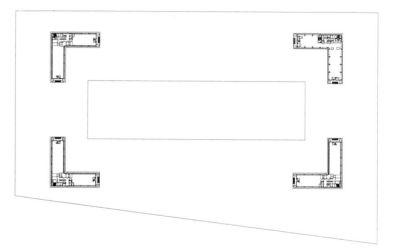

desk at home. Digital data storage media are gradually taking the place of original and often irreplaceable documents, to the great relief of curators. The multimedia department is developing an extensive media library whose collections include videos and CDs produced in France and worldwide.

Opposite and below:

Four depository towers, each nearly 80 metres tall, designed to resemble open books, surround an internal 28,680-square metre garden, creating not only a library of colossal stature but also an area of relaxation and contemplation beyond the reaches of the busy 13th arrondissement. The library reading rooms are situated in the six-storey base.

Above right:

Detail of the shallow wooden steps leading up to the library platform. Perrault has played off the warmth of natural building materials against the glazed façades of the towers, and he continues this idea by the use of low-tech wooden shutters to screen out sunlight.

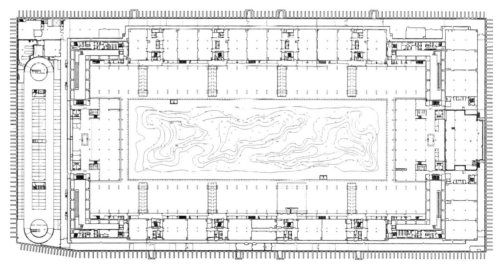

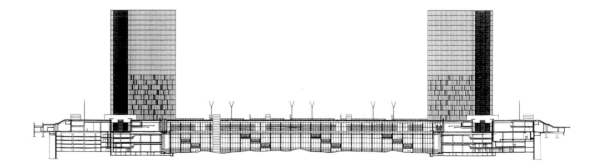

The research library faces the internal courtyard with its specially selected fully matured trees. Again there is a contrast between warmth and coldness, this time through the wooden detailing and the concrete structural supports.

The research library with custom-made lighting. The rich orange carpeting is laid in strips to catch the daylight, which is softly diffused through shuttered windows in contrast with the stark use of raw concrete and metallic fabric.

The reception area. Light that is already filtered through shutters is further softened by the insertion of large opaque glass panels.

The science and technology library is located under an acoustically designed flying saucer through which the garden can be reached.

UNIVERSITÄT II, ULM, GERMANY

ARCHITECT:
STEIDLE & PARTNER
1992–94

The south German town of Ulm witnessed the rise and fall of a famous twentieth-century academic institution: the Hochschule für Gestaltung (College of Design), whose democratic, functional rationalism made an important contribution to the history of design. So much for the past; in the early 1980s, ambitious plans were devised to set the scene for future achievements. These included a science complex, a joint venture combining state and private research centres, to be built on a hillside location close to the existing university.

Munich-based architects Steidle & Partner won the competition for the new engineering faculty, called Universität II, to house the departments of Electrotechnology, Biomedicine and Energy Technology. Their 400-metre-long complex has a comb-like structure and a total floor space of 47,560 square metres; it was built in two phases and completed in 1994. With its brightly coloured, anarchic appearance, this collage of laboratories, offices, clean-room areas, cafeteria and lecture halls flouts all the conventions usually associated with the sober business of scientific research. "The idea is to describe, to transmit environments for creativity, for real-life, vigorous work. A clear concept, many-layered in its realisation. Not a world for specialists, but more an indicator of the closeness of art and science" (Otto Steidle).

This unruly wooden research complex has shown itself to be a remarkable experiment, supplying definitive proof that progressive technologies can be at home even in the simplest hut. The building costs were low, the functional requirements were solved in a pragmatic way, and the interior spaces are easily adapted for different uses. The plants and bushes of the building's natural setting run wild beneath the raised-level wings and over the façades. For all the apparent arbitrariness of its constructional methods and materials, the complex observes the simple and vital prescriptions of fire regulations: supply ducts and cable networks run though the concrete cellars; laboratories are housed in the steel construction above this; only the upper storeys (for offices) and the towers are built entirely of wood. The high-level safety requirements are fulfilled without detracting from the creative spaces of the design.

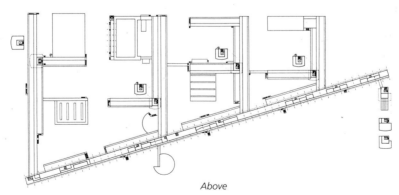

Above
Site-plan of the research complex.

Opposite
The brightly coloured, prefabricated look of Steidle & Partner's design is in direct contrast to the usual sober approach to scientific research establishments. The building is located in a zone between town and country and is fully landscaped with bushes, plants and water features.

The architect aimed to demonstrate
how progressive technology can be at
home in the most simple construction.
The top administrative offices are
constructed of wood. The interior
passageways remind one of a crude
but friendly workshop atmosphere.

PHOENIX PUBLIC LIBRARY, PHOENIX, USA

ARCHITECT/INTERIOR DESIGNER:
BRUDER DWL ARCHITECTS
1995

Over the decades the desert city of Phoenix grew too fast to allow for the development of arts facilities: all efforts were focused on building the necessary infrastructure. Now the city is making up for lost time, with a vitality and enthusiasm entirely in keeping with its dynamic community. A substantial arts quarter is being created in downtown Phoenix, including two new museums as well as the Public Library completed in 1995. Local architect Will Bruder was commissioned to design the library (which has more than 30,200 square metres of floor space), with the very modest budget of $27 million (£17.4 million). His design combines the pragmatic and the visionary, bridging the gap between local colour and international style: "The originality of the new Public Library is its celebration of an urban place in a beautiful desert setting. The solution combines confidence in the future with illusions, not imitations, of the historical past. It displays the romance of the West's natural beauty" (Will Bruder).

The architect's skill lies in his ability to transform necessity into metaphor. The rust-red, partially ribbed copper panelling of the east-west façades provides an abstract reference to the rock formations of Arizona. The transparency of the fully glazed north-south façades is a homage to the modern age, with computer-controlled metal blinds and airy textile sails forming an elaborate grid design. The building's simple mode of construction using concrete sections is similar to that of multi-storey warehouses. All service pipes are hidden away behind the massive, curved, red panels along the sides of the building (Bruder has described these panels, evocatively, as saddle bags). This arrangement meant that the open-plan five storeys could be arranged at will, interrupted only by the "Crystal Canyon" (Bruder) of the central glass atrium which cuts through the building.

The different departments within the library reflect the coexistence of the book, the traditional medium of information storage, and the new electronic media. The Media Library is on the ground floor, alongside an auditorium, a cafeteria and a children's library. On the first floor are the periodicals area and computer-based catalogues; the second houses book stacks, administrative offices and the computer centre; the third has the rare books collections and seminar rooms. Right at the top, on the fourth floor (which is nearly twice the height of the others), is the large reading room: a magnificent hangar of corrugated metal. The pillars taper towards, and end some distance below, the metal roof, which is supported by fine metal struts.

Opposite:
The north and south façades are fully glazed and protected from the fierce desert daylight by mechanically controlled metal blinds and prehensile fabric sails. The curved roof is supported by concrete sheets which are attached to the "saddlebags" west and east. These flank the main volume of the building and are clad in copper, used deliberately as a reference to the red stone of the Arizona desert.

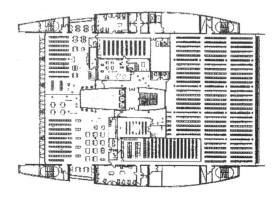

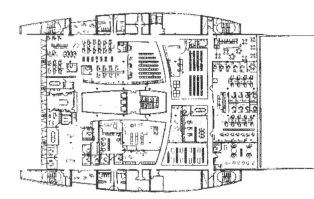

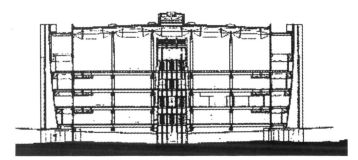

Left:
East-west section shows the top-lit "Crystal Canyon" running through the centre of the building. The "saddle-bags" to the west and east contain the service elements including exit stairs, leaving the main floor plans for exclusive library-related use.

Below left:

The reading room on the top floor is covered by a suspended ceiling strung from rigging supported by columns at key points. It is lit by integrated skylights placed directly over these structures and also by borrowed light entering from the glazed atrium at one end.

Below right:

The architect nicknamed the atrium "Crystal Canyon". It contains glass lifts which climb the north wall.

NEWMAN LIBRARY AND TECHNOLOGY CENTER, NEW YORK, USA

INTERIOR DESIGNER:
DAVIS, BRODY & ASSOCIATES
1994

Today, the former headquarters of the Metropolitan Street Railway Corporation is one of New York's most progressive information centres. Baruch College, part of City University, converted this 100-year-old building into its new library, equipped with all the latest electronic research equipment. Its name reflects the fact that the traditional book library has become a networked multimedia information provider.

Behind the building's restored stone façade the New York architects Davis, Brody & Associates created a prototype for this new type of library, covering nine storeys and 35,500 square metres. The design brief stipulated that the provision of knowledge should be combined with the experience of learning: this "teaching library" introduces the students to the new information and communications technologies; using the library as a study aid in itself becomes an educational process. On the ground floor is the Media Center; users enter through automatic entrance gates using their student pass. The centre has more than one hundred multimedia terminals for academic research using digital storage media (CD-ROM, Video CDs) or on-line databases.

The collections of books and periodicals take up the four storeys above this, but electronics has also found its way into this traditional library area. At workstations here readers can access City University's central information network, as well as other local networks or inter-regional data services. On the sixth floor is the Computing and Technology Center, which houses over 400 computers, ranging from Power Macs to mainframe computers used for intensive research projects. Even the seventh floor is not free of computer terminals, although here they are restricted to the administrative offices and conference rooms. The rest of this storey is an airy, sparsely furnished lounge, an "indoor campus" where students can take a break from books and computer screens.

Opposite:

The former headquarters of the New York Cable Car Corporation was turned into a high-tech library.

Bottom right:

Over nine storeys the building contains the Media Center, four floors of the Williams and Anita Newman Library, student administrative services, the Baruch Computing and Technology Center and a Conference Center.

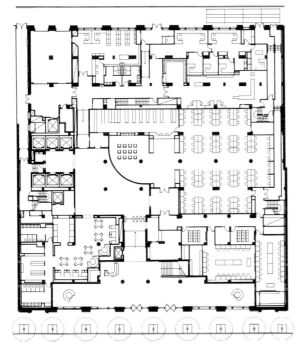

First floor plan

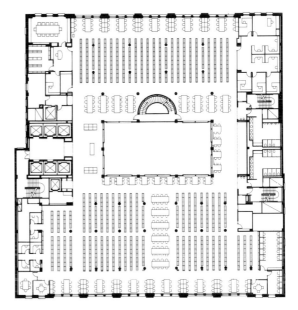

Fourth-floor plan

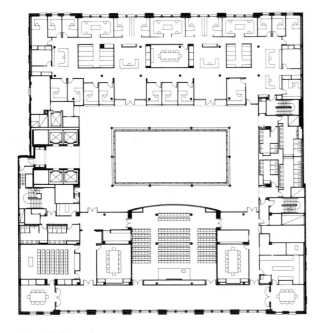

Seventh-floor plan

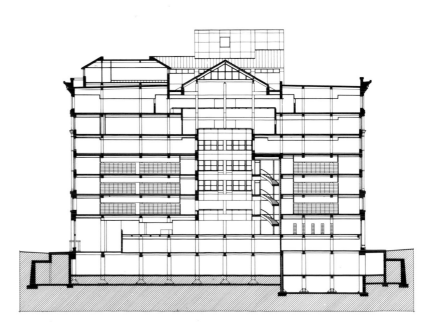

Right:

The Baruch Computing Center is situated on the sixth floor. It is lined with rows of computer workstations, all equipped with the latest technology. In a lab-like atmosphere, students who do not have a computer terminal of their own now have a viable alternative.

Below:

Reading rooms are equipped with laptop sockets for electronic work and research.

Opposite:

The top-lit atrium rises through the centre of the complex. The communal spaces, with cherrywood panelling, refer to traditional qualities of educational facilities and avoid the cold appearance of high-tech science factories.

MULTIMEDIA INFORMATION CENTRE, UEDA, JAPAN

ARCHITECT/INTERIOR DESIGNER:
**DENTSU/UNITÉS
ARCHITECTS & PLANNERS**
1994

The Japanese Ministry of International Trade and Industry (MITI) is envied by many other governments for its achievements. However, its activities extend beyond the promotion of economic interests: innovation also stands high on its agenda, and its efforts are not only directed at large companies. Among MITI's major decentralized initiatives is the creation of information centres which make the multimedia technologies of the future available to smaller companies and individuals. One of these centres is based in the Research Park in the town of Ueda. The austerely elegant wooden building, with its extended, shallow metal roof, might easily be a golf clubhouse. It nestles into the green landscape around it, redefining the local architectural tradition in a contemporary style. The designers of Japanese advertising group Dentsu described the project in the following terms: "The design itself emphasizes harmony and growth. Our objective is to design a way to combine the high-tech image of a multimedia information centre with an image of an environment that encourages human creativity."

Dentsu's marketing professionals collaborated with the architects of Unités to create an architectural shell that could be modified and adapted internally for a variety of functions. Its main purpose was to bring the digital revolution to Ueda: in the words of local mayor Etsuo Takeshita, "Our goal is to promote information-related skills in this area, and help create a concentration of high-level multimedia expertise". The two-storey L-shaped building is a demonstration area, training site and production studio rolled into one, with a floor space of 2,000 square metres. Permanent and temporary exhibitions display the latest hardware and software products, with the close cooperation of the relevant manufacturers. The auditorium, with its large projection screen, has room for more than 200 people. Basic information is available on CD-ROMs in an electronic library. The centre offers introductory courses on system and programme applications. In the studio, called the "digital factory", high-performance workstations can be used round the clock for developing multimedia products. To ensure that all these technologies did not produce a cold and soulless environment, Japan's largest cartoon design group created an animated mascot with companions. The multimedia mascot, Sarotubi Kid, guides even beginners through the perils of cyberspace.

Opposite:

The Multimedia Centre is situated in a green and leafy suburb of Ueda. The client's brief was to combine the high-tech image of a multimedia information centre with the image of an environment that encourages creativity. Dentsu have composed an understated building which belies the activities that take place within. Warmth is added to the predominantly painted wattle walls by touches of copper and reflective aluminium panels.

Drawings from top:

Floor plan. The two-storey L-shaped structure contains an auditorium which can seat 200 people, as well as an open space used for exhibitions. This can be altered by means of sliding partitions. There is also a library, seminar rooms and a "digital factory".

Section of roof feature. The extended shallow metal roof is supported on a wooden frame of laminated red pine, and this is tethered to the ground by way of wooden poles which articulate the profile of the design (*right*).

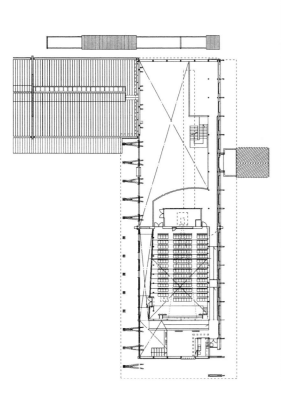

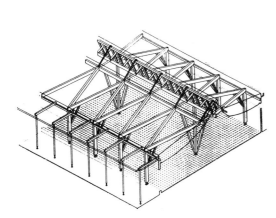

Permanent and temporary exhibitions display the latest hardware and software products.

View from the exhibition area towards the auditorium.

The Digital Factory uses high-powered workstations to create multimedia products.

The Monitor Space on the second floor houses a library of CD ROMs and multimedia personal computers.

SCIENCE, INDUSTRY AND BUSINESS LIBRARY, NEW YORK, USA

INTERIOR DESIGNER:
GWATHMEY SIEGEL & ASSOCIATES
1996

When the traditional New York department store B. Altman closed down in 1990, Manhattan was threatened with the loss of more than just a respected retail business. A whole block between Madison Avenue and Fifth Avenue seemed likely to fall prey to conventional property developers, who would pack in the maximum number of bland offices behind the protected façades. Happily these fears did not materialize: the New York Public Library decided to use the building for its new science and business division. The Science, Industry and Business Library (SIBL for short) was not intended to become an ordinary specialist library: it was given a budget of $100 million (£64.5 million) to fund its quantum leap into the multimedia world. Renowned local architects Gwathmey Siegel & Associates were commissioned to design the project and described their approach as follows: "The library is transformed into an interactive resource for the Information Age, retaining the building's classic integrity while incorporating the most advanced computer technologies into its infrastructure. The contrast between the 1906 Renaissance Revival façade and the elegant modernist interior reflects the balance between the library's nineteenth-century origins as a temple of wisdom and its twenty-first-century role as an emporium of rapidly changing information."

On a floor space of 23,000 square metres, their building resolves these considerable challenges in exemplary fashion, setting new standards in terms of both functionality and style. The architects created a successful, high-quality synthesis of library and on-line information centre, designed for use by a broad public. An inspired pragmatism prevails over the whole design. The ground floor and basement on Madison Avenue were converted into a public library area, while the library's stock of 1.5 million books disappeared into five densely packed archive storeys in the depths of the former department store. Administrative offices are arranged along the front of the building. The entrance leads into a public foyer which occupies the basement and ground-floor levels. Old arched ceilings were exposed and original pillars

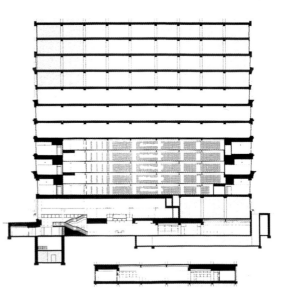

Opposite top:

The old site of the B. Altman department store is the new home for New York's SIB Library.

Opposite bottom:

Section. The main facilities are housed in the first two floors and in the basement. Offices surround the stacking storeys in the upper floors.

Below:

From street level, visitors reach the reception lobby below by stairs and lifts.

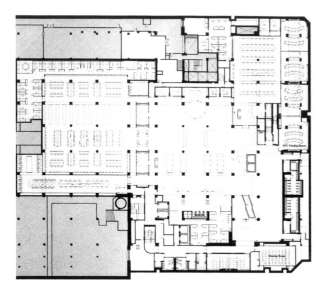

Lower level

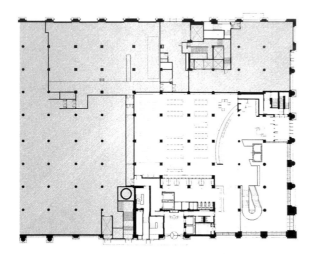

Street level

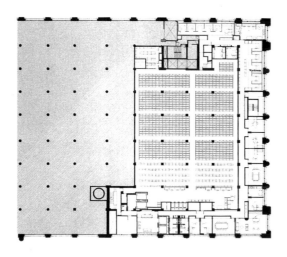

Level one

were preserved. Electronic aids are everywhere, but they are never obtrusive. "For those who can't afford computers and the other expensive tools needed to take advantage of the latest forms of information, the new library opens a door to the information highway", explains Elizabeth Rohatyn, chairman of the board of trustees.

A computerized signposting system guides visitors around the library. All the 500 reading desks are equipped with laptop sockets and modems for Internet access, and there are 95 fixed research terminals (use of the network is free of charge). All divisions of the New York Public Library have the same user-friendly software for the on-line catalogue and reference systems. The Electronic Information Center helps with specialist research, while business users can obtain advice, documentation and software solutions from the Small Business Information Center. The Electronic Training Center offers regular computer training courses for the uninitiated, free of charge. Only one process has escaped computerization: book order slips are still sent to the book stacks using a pneumatic dispatch system, just as in the old days.

Opposite top:
The interior design features solid standards and evokes civic qualities not only in the reading areas.

Opposite bottom:
McGraw Information Services Center with rows of computer stations offers free access to library resources and network services.

The following photographic credits are given, with page numbers in brackets:

Alsop & Störmer Architects, Albert Bridge House, 127 Albert Bridge Road, London SW11 4PL, UK

William Alsop founded his own architectural practice in 1980. He was born in 1947 in Northampton and studied at the Architectural Association in London (1968–73), following which he spent periods in the studios of Maxwell Fry, Cedric Price and Roderick Ham. He is currently Professor of Architecture at the University of Vienna and has been associated in various teaching capacities with the Royal Melbourne Institute of Technology, the San Francisco Institute of Art, St Martin's School of Art, London, the Bremen Academy of Art and Music and Hanover University. His major projects vary in scale from museum and urban planning designs in Hamburg, to the Real World Leisure Park in Sydney and a retail and housing development in Normandy. Recent projects include the CrossRail platform for Paddington Station, London, and the Regional Headquarters and Metro Station in Marseilles, as well as studies for the Blackfriars Railway Bridge and the Hungerford Pedestrian Bridge in London. William Alsop is a member of the Royal Institute of British Architects, Fellow of the Royal Society of Arts, a Bernard Webb Scholar (Rome), and was awarded the William van Allen Medal for Architecture.

Anderson/Schwartz Architects, 180 Varick Street, 15th Floor, New York 10014, New York, USA

Anderson/Schwartz is an award-winning, multi-disciplinary firm which has achieved international recognition for its innovative solutions in the workplace, often combining straightforward simplicity of traditional building solutions with the complexity of more obvious and studied design. Frederic Schwartz and Ross Anderson received their Master of Architecture degrees from Harvard University in 1978, having graduated from the University of California, Berkeley, and Stanford University respectively. Prior to founding their own company in 1984, Schwartz was director of Venturi, Rauch and Scott Brown, and Anderson was an associate at MLTW/Turnbull Associates. They have both taught architectural design at Princeton, Harvard, Yale, Columbia, Pennsylvania and Miami Universities as well as at the University of North Carolina, Carnegie-Mellon Technical University, and Parsons School of Design. Recent schemes include the much-praised SMA Video production facility; Predictive Systems Offices, Reach Network, and Isaac Mizrahi & Co. headquarters. They are currently working on a 50,000-square-foot office interior for *New York* magazine, the reconstruction of the 15,000-square-foot Bumble & Bumble salon, Long Island, and residences on Long Island.

Architect 5, 4-10-3-5F Yoga, Setagaya-ku, Tokyo 158, Japan

Architect 5 was founded in 1986 and today consists of four partners – the founding members Takeo Matsuoka, Hidetsugu Horikoshi and Junichi Kawamura who all trained at Tokyo University of Fine Arts, Department of Architecture, as well as Hirotaka Kidosaki who joined the group in 1993. All four had previously worked in the offices of Kenzo Tange Associates. Since their collaboration started they have been awarded the Ministry

of Trade and Industry Award (1989); the Sapporo Urban Landscape Award (1989); the Japan Society of Architects Award (1993); and the Japan Townscape Award (1994).

Arquitectonica, 2151 Lejeune Road, Suite 300, Coral Gables, Florida 33134, USA

Arquitectonica was founded in 1977 by Laurinda Spear (FAIA) and Bernardo Fort-Brescia, who received Master's degrees from Columbia and Harvard Universities respectively. Today, the Florida-based architectural practice is well known worldwide for its inventive use of colour and form, and has offices in Miami, New York, San Francisco and Chicago. As well as extensive work in Miami, projects within the last ten years include the Taipei Fine Arts Museum, Taiwan (1990); Center for Innovative Technology, Virginia (1990); the Gallery MA, Tokyo (1993), and the Banque de Luxembourg (1994). Both partners are in demand by professional, civic and academic groups as lecturers, and the American Institute of Architects has published a book dedicated to their work. The firm has received awards for design from the AIA and *Progressive Architecture*. Current schemes include the United States Embassy in Lima and a Performing Arts Centre and Urban Complex in Dijon, France.

Aukett Associates, 2 Great Eastern Wharf, Parkgate Road, London SW11 4NP, UK

The Aukett Group was founded in 1972, becoming Aukett Associates plc in 1988. Since this time the practice has affiliated with companies in Berlin, Amsterdam, Brussels, Dublin, Milan and Paris, and offers design consultancy services to corporate, public and domestic clients. Recent projects include the British Airways Compass Centre at Heathrow Airport which won the Civic Trust award in 1996, and the Proctor & Gamble Headquarters in Brooklands which in 1996 was named the MIPIM European Office of the Year and received the RIBA award for the South-East region.

Bernhard Blauel Architects, 37 Claylands Road, London SW8 1NX, UK

Bernard Blauel trained in Germany, where he started his career in architecture and interior design. Postgraduate studies were undertaken at the Architectural Association, London in 1976–77 and he set up his own studio in London in 1986. He occasionally teaches and lectures at various schools, including the Architecture Foundation, London, Manchester University, Edinburgh University, the University of North London and Harvard University. Selected projects include partial refurbishment of the German Embassy, London, St Giles Hospital after-care centre, various residential schemes, and offices in Germany, the UK and the USA, as well as the Cyberia Cafés in Paris, Manchester and Ealing, and an art gallery in Birmingham.

William P. Bruder Ltd, 1314 West Circle Mountain Road, New River, Arizona 85027, USA

William Bruder was born in Wisconsin in the 1940s. He is a self-taught architect, having turned down a place at IIT Architectural

School for the more practical training he received in the office of architect William Wenzler. He later studied sculpture at the University of Wisconsin. He undertook a year's travel and research programme in Arizona, where he worked with both Bruce Goff and Paolo Scolari before moving to Detroit to take a place with Gunnar Birkerts. He returned to Arizona, and eventually opened his own architectural practice in 1974, building his own studio where he has been ever since, apart from a year spent at the Academy of Rome in 1987. To date he has completed more than 150 projects, starting with small domestic schemes and culminating in the Phoenix Public Library.

Coop Himmelblau, Seilerstätte 16/11a, Vienna A-1010 Austria

Coop Himmelblau was founded in 1968 by Wolf D. Prix (b. 1942 in Vienna) and Helmut Swiczinsky (b. 1944 in Poznan, Poland). The firm has worked on a series of study and building projects in the fields of architecture, design and the arts. It has become well known for its open, avant-garde architecture, and has participated in many international exhibitions, including the 1988 Museum of Modern Art "Deconstructivist" architecture show and a solo exhibition at the Georges Pompidou Centre, Paris in 1993. During the last five years it has become increasingly involved in large-scale projects such as the Paris Melun-Senart City Planning Scheme; the Ronacher Theatre Renovation Project in Vienna and the Hygiene Museum in Dresden. In 1988, Prix and Swiczinsky opened an office in Los Angeles, working on West Coast/Pacific Rim projects which include a five-storey restaurant/bar in Japan. The office is currently working on several design proposals and has recently completed projects such as the Academy of Fine Arts in Munich, the UFA Cinema Centre in Dresden and apartment buildings in Austria.

John Csaky of Button/Csaky, 19 Store Street, London WC1E 7DH, UK

John Csaky is the principal of Button/Csaky. He attended the Portsmouth School of Art and later studied at the Royal College of Art, London, where he received a Master of Arts degree in environmental design. Since that time he has worked for Fitch as its Seville office director and director of its leisure division, and for the Milton Keynes Development Corporation, where he designed and ran the 50,000-capacity Milton Keynes Bowl. He has handled the lighting of the Isle of Wight Music Festival, special effects for a Walt Disney film première, and has designed information kiosks for the Quinto Centario in Spain, and a sculpture studio for the late Dame Elisabeth Frink. In 1988, he designed exhibition pavilions for the British contingent at Expo in Brisbane, and, in 1992, three pavilions for Puerto Rico at Expo in Seville. He is particularly concerned with the successful combination of entertainment, educational and intellectual elements, a preoccupation evident in the Chinese Galleries at the Victoria and Albert Museum, London and at the Futurevision exhibition for Granada Television. He is currently involved in a wildlife project.

Dai'chi-Kobo Associates, 5-9-12, 408 Minami-Aoyama, Minato-ku, Tokyo 107, Japan
Dai'chi-Kobo Associates was founded in 1960. Since then it has become a well-established architectural practice nationally, winning the Architectural Institute of Japan Award in 1971 (Saga Prefectural Museum), and in 1981 (National Research Institute for Pollution Studies and Hideyo Tsukamoto Memorial Hall and Art-Information Centre, Osaka). The practice has also been the recipient of the Minister of Education Award for Promotion of the Arts (1979), and the Arts Academy of Japan Award (1982). Its most recent honour was the Building Constructors' Society Award for the Tokyo Metropolitan University in 1992. The firm is currently working on the Kumamoto Sports Dome.

Davis, Brody & Associates, LLP Architects, 315 Hudson Street, New York, NY 10013, USA
Davis, Brody & Associates was founded in 1952 and is involved in the design of academic and institutional buildings, corporate research and industrial facilities, corporate offices, and housing. They have received over one hundered major international design awards including the prestigious American Institute of Architects Firm Award in 1975. Major schemes include campuses at Harvard, Yale, Princeton, Brown, Columbia and Cornell Universities; the campus master plan and architecture for the new University of Science and Technology in Zimbabwe; Corning Glass Works; design of a mixed-use building for the 12 cultural institutions that make up the Lincoln Center for Performing Arts; the master plan for New York's World Trade Center public and retail spaces and the multi-purpose research tower for the Mount Sinai School of Medicine in New York.

Dentsu Inc., 1–11 Tsukiji, Chuo-ku, Tokyo 104, Japan
Dentsu Inc. is the world's largest advertising company. It was founded in 1901 by Hoshiro Mitsunaga and today employs over 6,000 people, maintaining 32 offices in Japan, 6 offices overseas, and subsidiaries and affiliates in 45 cities and 35 countries around the world.

Atelier Christian de Portzamparc, 1 rue de l'Aude, 75014 Paris, France
Christian de Portzamparc was born in 1944 and studied architecture at the Ecole Nationale Supérieure des Beaux-Arts in Paris. His early research into the "theory of the city" which states that architecture should relate to its urban situation through a sensitive and pragmatic, yet new and modern, approach has influenced the work of his practice to date. His early designs include the water-tower at Marne la Vallée; the rue des Hautes Formes (1969); and the urban plan for the residential block "La Petite Roquette" in Paris. The design of the latter formed part of de Portzamparc's Programme for New Architecture (PAN VII, 1974). The Conservatoire Erik Satie (1983) was the first in a series of designs devoted to music and dance, and was followed by the Ecole de Danse de L'Opéra de Paris (1983); the Opéra Bastille; and the Cité de la Musique which, standing at the entrance to the Parc de la Villette, is one

of Mitterrand's Grands Travaux. During the 1980s, de Portzamparc also worked on interiors such as the Café Beaubourg and the boutique for Emmanuel Ungaro in Paris, but in recent years he has returned to his interest in urban development, and in 1991 an exhibition was held in Tokyo dedicated to his urban projects. Recent schemes include a cultural centre in Rennes, the headquarters of DDB Newham Worldwide and law courts in Grasse. Christian de Portzamparc has held various teaching posts, including a Professorship at the Ecole Spéciale d'Architecture in Paris and he has received the Commandeur de l'Ordre des Arts et des Lettres, the Grand Prix National d'Architecture, the Pritzker Prize and the Grand Prix d'Architecture de la Ville de Paris, in recognition of his achievements.

Ecart, 111 rue Saint-Antoine, 75004 Paris, France
The Ecart Group was founded in 1978 by Andrée Putman, who was born in Paris and studied music under François Poulenc before becoming first a journalist and later a design consultant for the mass-market chain Prisunic. She was co-founder of "Créateurs et Industriels", which introduced the work of Issey Miyake and Jean Muir, among others, to France. The Ecart practice is divided into three specific disciplines. Ecart SA is the design office, specializing in interior and product design, ranging from hotels to boutiques, corporate offices to private houses, and museums to governmental offices. Notable designs include the Office of the Minister of Culture, Paris (1984); Ebel Headquarters, Basle (1985); Morgans Hotel, New York (1985); and the Im Wasserturm Hotel, Cologne (1990). Ecart International re-edits furniture and objects by designers such as Eileen Gray and Mariano Fortuny, and edits designs by Ecart SA. Andrée Putman licensing division designs objects which are distributed throughout the world, including rugs, upholstery fabrics, tableware and bathroom accessories. Recent projects by Ecart SA include the Cartier Foundation exhibition areas (1993); the Sheraton Hotel, Paris-Roissy (1994); the Bally Boutiques concept (1993–94); and the brand images of Baccarat and Swarovski.

Erick van Egeraat, Calandstraat 23, 3016 CA, Rotterdam, The Netherlands
Erick van Egeraat was born in 1956 in Amsterdam. He graduated from the Architectural Department of the Technical University of Delft in 1984. He co-founded Mecanoo architects in 1983 and worked there until 1995, when he decided to set up his own practice. He has lectured at various academic establishments throughout the Low Countries and in Germany, and more recently at the Royal Institute of British Architects, London (1995); the Junta de Sevilla (1995); the Oxford School of Architecture (1995), and the Staatliche Akademie der Bildenden Künste, Stuttgart (1996). He is an Honorary Member of the Bund Deutsche Architekten, and has received national acclaim for his designs, being recommended for a design award in 1995 for his work on the ING Bank in Budapest. His work has been the subject of numerous articles and reviews.

Fitch & Co., Commonwealth House, Number One, New Oxford Street, London WC1A 1WW, UK
Fitch & Co. is the London-based branch of Fitch RS, which also has offices in the United States, and affiliates in Europe and the Far East. The practice is concerned with interior design, graphic communication, product design and architecture. Major clients include Coca Cola, Reebok, Midland Bank, Hamleys, Woolworths, Virgin Atlantic, Disney Development Corporation, and the Science Museum and Victoria and Albert Museum. Recent projects include the Virgin Atlantic Conservatory (Heathrow Terminal 3); Dillons Bookstore (Birmingham); offices for the London-based newspaper *Loot*, and a corporate identity scheme for London buses.

Fletcher Priest Architects, 23–27 Heddon Street, London, W1R 8RA, UK
Fletcher Priest Architects was founded in 1978 by Michael Fletcher and Keith Priest who had previously worked as associates in a European design consultancy. The practice has offices in London and Cologne and has completed projects in Singapore, Tel Aviv, Stockholm, France, Holland, Germany, Ireland and the USA. Their expertise covers three areas: master-planning, architecture and interior design, and notable projects include Luton Arts and Media Centre; Sony Pictures Europe, London; the London Planetarium refurbishment and the PowerGen offices which was awarded Office of the Year in 1996.

Sir Norman Foster and Partners, Riverside Three, 22 Hester Road, London SW11 4AN, UK
Sir Norman Foster was born in Manchester, England in 1935, and studied architecture and city planning at the University of Manchester and at Yale University. He established Team 4 in 1963 – with his late wife, Wendy, and Su and Richard Rogers – and founded Foster Associates in 1967. Today he works from a studio on the south bank of the River Thames and has other offices in Glasgow, Berlin, Frankfurt, Hong Kong and Tokyo. He is internationally famous for his high-tech designs, many of which have resulted directly from competitions, such as the Hong Kong and Shanghai Bank (1979–86), and Stansted Airport (1981–89). Projects include the Sackler Galleries at the Royal Academy of Arts, London, which was named RIBA Building of the Year in 1993; the Centre d'Art/Cultural Centre, Nîmes; the remodelling of the Reichstag, Berlin; ITN Headquarters, London; Cranfield University Library; the new wing of the Josslyn Arts Museum, Omaha, Nebraska; and the University of Cambridge Law Faculty. Master plans include the King's Cross development, London. Among Foster's current projects are the new headquarters for the Commerzbank in Frankfurt, development of the Imperial War Museum in Duxford, Cambridge, the redevelopment of the British Museum, London, and an airport at Chek Lap Kok for Hong Kong (covering an area of 1,248 hectares, this is the largest project in the world). Foster received a knighthood in the Queen's Birthday Honours in 1991, and his work has won over sixty awards and citations. He is a well-known figure on the international lecturing circuit. Although primarily concerned

with large-scale architectural projects, Foster is also involved in furniture design.

Frank O. Gehry & Associates, 1520-B Cloverfield Blvd, Santa Monica, California 90404, USA

Frank O. Gehry is Principal-in-Charge of Frank O. Gehry and Associates Inc., which he established in 1962. He studied architecture at the University of Southern California and city planning at Harvard University's Graduate School of Design. His architectural career spans four decades and has involved public and private buildings in America, Japan and most recently Europe, including the Vitra Furniture Manufacturing Facility and Design Museum in Germany, and the American Cultural Center in Paris. He won the Pritzker Architecture Prize in 1989 and has been named a trustee of the American Academy in Rome. His work has been featured in numerous professional publications and national and international trade journals and can be found in permanent museum collections. In 1986, a major retrospective exhibition of his designs entitled "The Architecture of Frank O. Gehry" was organized by the Walker Art Center, Chicago and travelled throughout the USA. Recent selected projects include the Chiat/Day office building in Venice, California; the Disney Concert Hall in Los Angeles; an office building for Vitra International in Basel; a museum in Bilbao; a retail complex in Barcelona; an art museum in Minnesota; a children's museum in Boston; the EMR Communication and Technology Centre in Bad Oeynhausen; the University of Toledo Center for the Visual Arts, Ohio; and the design of the Concord Pavilion in Concord, California. The firm has recently won an invited competition to design a mixed-use building on the Pariser Platz, adjacent to the Brandenburg Gate in Berlin, and is also involved in smaller-scale residential projects and furniture design.

Michael Graves, 341 Nassau Street, Princeton, New Jersey 08540, USA

Michael Graves was born in Indianapolis and received his architectural training at the University of Cincinnati and Harvard University. Since the formation of his practice in 1964, he has become an influential figure and has produced designs for over 200 projects, including office buildings, hotels and convention centres, private residences, sports facilities, institutional buildings, retail spaces, theatres, libraries, museums and other cultural facilities. Through his affiliated company Graves Design he has produced an extensive collection of furniture and consumer products, collaborating with manufacturers such as Alessi, Arkitektura, Swid Powell, Baldinger and Atelier International. Major architectural projects include the Walt Disney World Swan and Dolphin Hotels, Orlando, Florida; the Disney Company Corporate Headquarters, Burbank, California; the Crown American Offices; the Whitney Museum of American Art in Johnstown; a master plan for the Detroit Institute of Arts; the Denver Public Library; and the Clark County Library in Las Vegas. Current schemes encompass work in Japan and Taiwan, as well as the corporate headquarters for Thomson Consumer Electronics in Indianapolis; an office building for the Ministry of Culture in The Hague; the

Pittsburgh Cultural Trust's Public Theater; and condominiums on Miami Beach. Graves has designed the *Life* 1996 Dream House and has recently been selected as the principal designer of the US Courthouse Annexe in Washington DC. He is a member of the American Institute of Architects and has received many awards, including fifteen *Progressive Architecture* awards and nine American Institute of Architects National Honor awards. Graves is the Schirmer Professor of Architecture at Princeton University, where he has taught since 1962.

Nicholas Grimshaw and Partners Ltd, 1 Conway Street, Fitzroy Square, London W1P 5HA, UK

Nicholas Grimshaw founded his own practice in 1980, having already won acclaim for his industrial architecture with buildings for Citroen, Zanussi, Herman Miller and BMW. Today, the firm handles a wider range of projects, including sports and leisure complexes, commercial and retail buildings and schemes in the fields of television and radio. Notable buildings include the Oxford Ice Rink; the *Financial Times* Printing Works; completion of a new research facility for Xerox Research; the Combined Operations Centre for British Airways at Heathrow; the RAC Regional Headquarters in Bristol; and the International Passenger Terminal for the Channel Tunnel at Waterloo. In 1982, the practice won the Sports Council's national competition for the design of standardized sports halls throughout the UK, twenty-four of which have now been built. Currently under construction is the Berlin Stock Exchange and Communication Centre; the new South Wing for Heathrow Terminal 3; the redevelopment of Manchester Airport's Terminal One; and a new headquarters building for Hutchinson Telecom in Darlington. Grimshaw believes that architectural form should reflect the function of a building, and his ergonomically-controlled designs have been the subject of many awards and commendations, including a number from the Civic Trust, the Department of the Environment, the Royal Institute of British Architects and the Royal Fine Art Commission. Grimshaw and Partners held two highly-acclaimed exhibitions in 1988 and 1993 at the Royal Institute of British Architects.

Gwathmey Siegel & Associates Architects, 475 Tenth Avenue, New York, NY 100018, USA

Gwathmey Siegel & Associates was founded in 1967 by Charles Gwathmey and Robert Siegel, who are both Fellows of the American Institute of Architects and recipients of the Medal of Honor from its New York Chapter. Charles Gwathmey studied at the University of Pennsylvania and Yale University and has held numerous teaching posts, including positions at Princeton and Columbia as well as visiting professorships at Yale and Harvard. Robert Siegel trained at the Pratt Institute and Harvard University. Their designs range in scale from arts and educational facilities and major corporate buildings to furniture systems and decorative art objects, and in 1982 the firm became the youngest architectural practice to be given the Firm Award, the highest accolade of the American Institute

of Architects. Recent projects include the Contemporary Resort Convention Center at Walt Disney World; additions to the faculties of Cornell University; The Busch Reisinger Museum and Fine Arts Library addition to the Fogg Museum at Harvard University; the restoration of and addition to Frank Lloyd Wright's Solomon R. Guggenheim Museum in New York; and the Science, Industry and Business Library at the New York Public Library. Works in progress include the Henry Art Museum at the University of Washington and the Physics Building at Princeton University, whilst those under development include the Rehabilitation and Biomedical Research Center at the State University of New York and the Supercomputer Faculty/Teaching Building at the University of California, San Diego.

Hellmuth, Obata + Kassabaum Inc., 211 North Broadway, One Metropolitan Square, Suite 600, St Louis, Missouri 63102–2231, USA

Hellmuth, Obata + Kassabaum was founded in 1955 and today employs over 1,300 people. Their area of expertise covers work for major corporations, developers, state and local agencies, sports facilities, hospital colleges and universities, the US government and governments in Canada, the Caribbean, Central and South America, the Middle East and Asia. The firm offers services in architecture, engineering, interior design, graphic design, planning, landscape architecture, facility programming/management and consulting. Gyo Obata FAIA is co-chairman of the firm. He received a Bachelor's degree in architecture in 1945 from Washington University and a Master's in architecture and urban design from the Cranbrook Academy of Art. He has Honorary PhDs from Washington University and the University of Missouri. George Hellmuth (now retired) received a Bachelor's and Master's degree from Washington University and also studied at the Ecole des Beaux Arts at Fontainebleau, France. He was awarded the Gold Medal Award by the St Louis Chapter of the AIA. George Kassabaum FAIA (d. 1982) also studied at Washington University. He served as a national president of the AIA in 1968–69 and as chancellor of the College of Fellows of the AIA in 1977–78. The current Senior Design Principal of HOK is Charles Davis FAIA, who studied Architecture and Design Administration at the University of California at Berkeley. He is the Director of the San Francisco Chapter of the American Institute of Architects and has taught at the University of Hawaii and the University of California at Berkeley. Selected projects include the Federal Reserve Bank in Minneapolis; the Los Angeles County Replacement Hospital; the Department of State at the US Embassy in Moscow; and a high-rise building for the Principal Life Insurance Company in Des Moines, Iowa.

Herzog & De Meuron Architekten, Rheinschanze 6, Basel CH-4056, Switzerland

The architectural firm Herzog & De Meuron was created in 1978 by Jacques Herzog (b. 1950) and Pierre de Meuron (b. 1950), and expanded to include two further partners, Harry Gugger and Christine Binswanger. Both Herzog and De Meuron received degrees in architecture from the

Eidgenössische Technische Hochschule in Zurich and together became assistants to Professor Dolf Schnelbli. They are currently visiting professors at Harvard University.

Holabird & Root, 300 West Adams Street, Chicago, Illinois 60606–5174, USA

Holabird & Root was founded in 1880, and a further office was opened a century later in Rochester, Minnesota. The company offers a range of services in engineering and interior and graphic design. Their clients range from corporate, education, and research and development organizations to institutions, health-care centres, industrial, financial and government bodies. Projects have ranged from small additions to renovations and large-scale new constructions. The company has received countless honours, most recently the AIA Chicago Award for the Motorola Customers' Center for Systems Integration and the AIA Chicago Distinguished Building Award for the School of Architecture and Urban Planning at the University of Wisconsin-Milwaukee.

Hans Hollein, Argentinierstrasse 36, 1040 Vienna 4, Austria

Hans Hollein was born in 1934 and studied at the Academy of Fine Arts in Vienna, the Illinois Institute of Technology in Chicago and the University of California at Berkeley where he obtained his Master of Architecture in 1960. He has been practising as an independent architect, planner and designer since 1964, whilst at the same time teaching, from 1967 to 1976, at the Düsseldorf Academy of Fine Arts and subsequently at the Academy of Applied Arts, Vienna. He is also Guest Professor at Washington, Yale and Ohio State Universities as well as at the University of California. He was the editor of *Bau*, a magazine for architecture and planning, from 1965 to 1970, and is also an architectural historian, specializing in the work of Rudolph M. Schindler. He achieved recognition in 1965 with the Retti Candleshop in Vienna. Since that time major projects have included the Museum of Glass and Ceramics, Tehran (1977–78); art museums in Mönchengladbach (1982) and Frankfurt (1991); the Haas Haus commercial building, Vienna (1985–90); the Banco Santander Headquarters, Madrid (1988–93); the EA Generali Headquarters, Bregenz (1988–93); Study Donau-City Access area (1993); and the showroom for Zumtobel LichtgesmbH, Vienna (1995–96). Designs under construction include the Salzburg Guggenheim Museum feasibility study, the Cultural Quarters of St Poelten, the new capital of Lower Austria and the headquarters of EA Generali, Vienna. Hollein has also undertaken many urban planning studies in Austria and Germany, and has designed products for manufacturers such as Franz Wittman, Alessi, Swid Powell, Knoll and Thonet. He has held innumerable one-man shows and has received both national and international awards, including the Award for Excellence in Planning and Design for the Banco Santander, Madrid by the *Architectural Record* (1995). He is an Honorary Member of the American Institute of Architects and the Royal Institute of British Architects, and a corresponding member of the Académie d'Architecture in Paris.

Michael Hopkins & Partners, 27 Broadley Terrace, London NW1 6LG, UK

Michael Hopkins & Partners was formed in 1976 and today has three directors, Sir Michael Hopkins, Patricia Hopkins and Bill Taylor. The practice is well known for its advanced building techniques which utilize modern materials such as lightweight fabric structures, steel and glass, and for its reinterpretation of traditional materials. It is also noted for its work with listed buildings such as Sir Albert Richardson's Bracken House, the Victoria and Albert Museum and Glyndebourne Opera House. Principal projects include the Hopkins' family house in Hampstead, London (1976); the Schlumberger Research Laboratories, Cambridge (1985); and Bedfont Lakes for MEPC (1992). Currently at the design stage are new parliamentary offices for the House of Commons. Michael Hopkins has been awarded a CBE for services to architecture. He is a Royal Academician, a commissioner with the Royal Institute of British Architects and Architectural Association Councils and a Trustee of the Thomas Cubitt Trust.

Kiessler + Partner Architekten, Mauerkircherstrasse 41, 81679 Munich, Germany

Kiessler + Partner was founded in 1962 in Munich by Uwe Kiessler (b. 1937) and Hermann Schultz (b. 1936). Kiessler graduated from the Berlin Academy of Art and today is Professor of Architecture and Planning at Munich Technical University. Notable projects include the Bayerische Rückversicherung headquarters and Soft Lab Technical Centre, Munich; Heliowatt, Berlin; the ERCO Technical Centre, Ludenscheid; and the Grüner & Jahr headquarters in Hamburg.

Francisco José Larrucea, Rios Rosas 5-4ºB, 28003 Madrid, Spain

Francisco José Larrucea was born in Bilbao, Spain in 1954. He undertook advanced architectural studies at the Higher School of Architecture in Madrid and specialized in design and construction. In 1984 he was chosen by competitive entry examination to work for the Department of Planning and Public Works of the Municipality of Madrid, staying there until he opened his own studio in 1989. Major works include a housing block consisting of 280 units in Granada; the Fuenlabrada Town Hall; restoration and extension of the Historical Public Record Office, Salamanca; and the National Data-Processing Centre and Urban Telephone Exchange for Telefonica de España SA. From 1987 to 1991 Larrucea was Associate Lecturer in architectural planning and design at the Higher School of Architecture in Madrid.

Lund & Slatto Arkitekter AS, Drammensveien 145 A, Postboks 69, Skoyen 0212, Oslo, Norway

Kjell Lund (b. 1927) and Nils Slatto (b. 1923) were born in Lillehammer and educated at the Technical University of Trondheim. In 1958 they won a design competition for the extension of an agricultural school which encouraged them to open their own architectural office. Throughout their career they have been concerned with the timber house and how this sits in the surrounding landscape, a concept which led them to develop their award-winning "Alhytta" prefabricated building system. This has been used in more than 4,000 buildings erected within the last twenty-five years. In the early 1970s, Lund and Slatto were awarded the contract for the extension of the National Gallery and the company was forced to expand. Major works from the 1980s onwards include the re-design of the Students Park and the Eidsvold Square in Oslo; the European Youth Centre in Strasbourg; the Christiania Bank Headquarters; and St Magnus Church. In 1989, the office was the only European firm invited by the World Bank to take part in the competition for their new Headquarters in Washington DC. Currently, Lund and Slatto are working on an architectural competition for a new military camp in Norway and have recently completed the VH-Huset newspaper offices in Oslo. The architects are Knights of the Order of St Olaf and Honourable Members of both the National Association of Norwegian Architects and the American Institute of Architects. They are widely published in the international press, have participated in architectural competition juries and lecture both at home and abroad.

Maki and Associates, 3-6-2 Nihonbashi, Chuo-ku, Tokyo, Japan

Maki and Associates was founded in 1965 by Fumihiko Maki. Maki was born in 1928 in Tokyo and received the degree of Bachelor of Architecture from the University of Tokyo. He continued his education in the USA, where he gained a Master of Architecture from the Cranbrook Academy of Art in 1953 and from Harvard University's Graduate School of Design in 1954. Before returning to Japan, Maki worked for Skidmore, Owings and Merrill in New York and for José Luis Sert, and in 1958, began teaching at Washington University in St Louis, at which time he received the Graham Foundation Travelling Fellowship. From 1962 to 1965 Maki served as an Associate Professor at Harvard University. In conjunction with his practice in Tokyo, Maki has served as Professor at the University of Tokyo and has taught and lectured extensively outside Japan at institutions including Columbia University, the University of California at Berkeley and the Technical University of Vienna. He is a member of the Japan Institute of Architects, and Honorary Fellow of both the American Institute of Architects and the Royal Institute of British Architects. Major completed projects to date include the National Museum of Modern Art, Kyoto (1986); the Tokyo Metropolitan Gymnasium, Tokyo (1990); YKK Research Centre, Tokyo (1993); the Center for the Arts, Yerba Buena Gardens, San Francisco; and the Isar Büropark, Munich (1994).

Richard Meier & Partners, 475 Tenth Avenue, New York, NY 10018, USA

Richard Meier was born in Newark, New Jersey in 1934. He studied architecture at Cornell University, then worked for architects Davis, Brody and Wisniewski in New York, followed by Skidmore, Owings and Merrill and Marcel Breuer. In the late 1950s and early 1960s he worked as an artist with Michael Graves, but set up his own architectural practice in New York in

1963. He has been Professor of Architecture at Harvard and Yale Universities as well as at the Cooper Union and in the 1970s was a member of the New York Five with Peter Eisenman, Michael Graves, Charles Gwathmey and John Hejduk, who advocated a modernist ideal strongly reminiscent of Le Corbusier's Cubist designs of the 1920s. Much of Meier's work at this time was derivative from previous twentieth-century designs, such as a tea-set for Alessi in the style of Malevich, and Hoffmanesque metalwork and ceramics for Swid Powell. Architectural work includes the Museum for Kunsthandwerk, Frankfurt; the High Museum, Atlanta; and the Getty Museum in Los Angeles. Recent projects include the City Hall and Central Library in The Hague, the Museum of Contemporary Art in Barcelona, the Museum of Television and Radio and the Gagosian Gallery, both in Los Angeles, and the Stadthaus in Ulm. In addition to the Getty Center, now under construction and due to open in 1998, Richard Meier & Partners is currently working on the United States Courthouses in Islip, Long Island and Phoenix, Arizona, and on the Ruregio Bank building in Basel, Switzerland. Richard Meier's work has been the subject of many solo exhibitions worldwide, and he has been the recipient of accolades such as the Arnold W. Brunner Memorial Prize, the Reynolds Memorial Award and the Pritzker Architecture Prize. In 1992, the French honoured Richard Meier as Commandeur des Arts et des Lettres, and in 1995 he was elected Fellow of the American Academy of Arts and Sciences. His life story has been the subject of a monograph and television film.

MET Studio, 6–8 Standard Place, Rivington Street, London EC2A OBE, UK

MET Studio is an award-winning design consultancy, specializing in exhibition and interior design for museum, corporate, government and leisure clients worldwide. The company was formed in 1982 and is led by Managing Director Alex McCuaig. Together with Museums Director, Deirdre Janson-Smith, and Leisure Director, Vic Kass, he supervises a team of concept planners, researchers, architects, interior, exhibit and graphic designers. MET Studio also works with sculptors and artists whose specially commissioned work is often integrated into projects. The Studio was awarded the 1995 Minerva Award for the Best Environment for its work on The Environment Theatre at the National Museum of Natural Science, Taiwan. In 1994 it won the Best Exhibition Award at the *DesignWeek* Awards for its work on the Sciences of Life Exhibition for the Wellcome Trust in London, and in 1996 it won the same award for the Telecom World project in Hong Kong. Science for Life also won the award for Best Education Initiative at the 1994 IBM Museum of the Year Awards, as well as a Special Award for Lighting Design. Recent projects include an exhibition for Hong Kong Telecom; a travelling exhibition for the Wellcome Trust; the National Museum of Prehistory, Taiwan; the refurbishment of the *QE2*; The Evolution of Plants exhibit at Kew Gardens; the Electronic Theatre at the Science Museum, London; and the D&AD Festival Exhibition 1995 at the Saatchi Gallery, London.

Nikken Sekkei, 4-6-2, Koraibashi, Chuo-ku, Osaka 541, Japan

Nikken Sekkei is the oldest and largest architectural firm in Japan. Originally founded in 1900, it was incorporated in its present form in 1950. The company has undertaken more than 13,000 projects in Japan as well as in forty countries worldwide, ranging from private museums to public housing and from high-tech factories to corporate headquarters. They have been the recipients of many national awards and have won numerous international competitions.

Nissoken Architects/Engineers, 1-34-14 Hatagaya, Shibuya-ku, Tokyo 151, Japan

Nissoken was founded in 1963. Affiliated to the Japan Architects Association, among other national organizations, it currently employs nearly 300 people and has nine subsidiary companies. The practice has received awards for many of its designs, most notably the NTT Building, Tokyo; the KDD Building, Tokyo; Toyama Modern Art Museum; Shizuoka University and the Higashiyama Sky Tower.

Jean Nouvel et Associés, 4 cité Griset, 75011 Paris, France

Jean Nouvel was born in 1945 in Lot et Garonne. He graduated from the Ecole Nationale Supérieure des Beaux Arts, Paris in 1971. His practice became internationally known following its design of the Institut du Monde Arabe, Paris in 1987. Other important projects include Hotel-Restaurant St James, Bordeaux (1989); the cultural centre at Mélun-Sénart (1986); the renovation of the Opera House in Lyons (1990); the Cartier Foundation, Paris (1994); and the Tour Sans Fin at La Défense, Paris. Jean Nouvel continues to produce successful furniture designs in collaboration with Ligne Roset, Ecart and other manufacturers. His architecture, which relies heavily on contemporary technology as a means of expression, has received many international design awards.

Pei Cobb Freed & Partners, 600 Madison Avenue, New York, NY 10022, USA

Ieoh Ming Pei was born in China in 1917. He moved to the USA to study architecture at the Massachusetts Institute of Technology, receiving a Bachelor of Architecture degree in 1940. He then studied at the Harvard Graduate School of Design under Walter Gropius, at the same time teaching in the faculty as Assistant Professor, and gained a Master's degree in 1946. In 1955, Pei formed I. M. Pei & Associates, which became I.M. Pei and Partners in 1966 and Pei Cobb Freed & Partners in 1989. The practice has designed over 150 projects in the USA and abroad, more than half of which have won awards and citations. As well as working for corporate and private investment clients, the practice has executed numerous commissions for public authorities and religious, educational and cultural institutions. Its most important buildings include the Bank of China, Hong Kong; the East West Wing of the National Gallery of Washington DC; the Grand Louvre in Paris and the United States Holocaust Memorial Museum,

Washington. Works recently completed are the Federal Triangle, Washington, and the San Francisco Main Public Library. Pei is a Fellow of the American Institute of Architects and a Corporate Member of the Royal Institute of British Architects, and in 1975 he was made a Member of the American Academy. He has honorary degrees from leading universities in the USA, Hong Kong and France. James Ingo Freed was the design architect for the San Francisco Public Library and is one of the three design principals of Pei Cobb Freed. He joined the offices in 1956, before which he worked in Chicago and New York, notably in the office of Mies van der Rohe. He received his architectural degree from the Illinois Institute of Technology and has received more than one hundred major awards including, most recently, the National Endowment for the Arts' National Medal of Arts, which was conferred by President Clinton in 1995.

Cesar Pelli & Associates Inc., 1056 Chapel Street, New Haven, CT 06510, USA

Cesar Pelli founded his own company in 1977, after a career which had already seen, amongst other projects, the construction of the Pacific Design Centre in Los Angeles and the US Embassy in Tokyo, and his appointment as Dean of the Yale University School of Architecture. Born in Argentina, and trained at the University of Tucuman, Pelli came to the USA with a scholarship to attend the University of Illinois. His belief that buildings should be "responsible citizens" is reflected in his concern for their suitability in terms of location and the city skyline. His first project after 1977 was the expansion and renovation of the Museum of Modern Art in New York, since which time the company has been the recipient of over eighty awards for design excellence, including an AIA citation for the World Financial Center and Winter Garden at Battery Park City, which has been cited as one of the ten best works of architecture completed after 1980. The AIA also awarded Cesar Pelli and Associates the 1989 Firm Award, in recognition of over a decade of leading-edge work in architectural design. Pelli has written extensively and his work has been widely published and exhibited.

Dominique Perrault, 26/34 rue Bruneseau, 75013 Paris, France

Dominique Perrault was born in Clermont-Ferrand in 1953 and studied architecture at the Ecole Nationale Supérieure des Beaux-Arts, Paris. He also gained a certificate of advanced studies in town-planning from the National School of Bridges and Roadways, Paris, as well as a Master's degree in History from the School of Advanced Studies in Social Sciences. Before opening his own studio in 1981, he worked for Martin van Treck, René Dottelonde and Antoine Grumbach, the consulting architects for the CAUE de la Mayenne. In 1983 Perrault was the winner of the "Programme for New Architecture" (PAN XII), France and the "Album of Young Architecture", Ministry of Housing, France, and in 1986 was made consultant architect for the Loiret District Council. Today he is also the consultant architect for the city of Nantes and is on the Council for Urban Planning in the city of Salzburg. Perrault has been a Member of the board of the French Institute of Architecture and of the Scientific and Technical Committee, ESA, in Paris since 1988. He has been the recipient of numerous awards in honour of his achievements, including second prize for town-planning from the Foundation of the Academy of Architecture for his project for the Bibliothèque de France. In 1993 he was awarded the Grand Prix National d'Architecture.

Gaetano Pesce Ltd, 543 Broadway, 5th Floor, New York, NY 10012, USA

Gateano Pesce was born in 1959 in La Spezia, Italy and studied in the architecture department of the University of Venice between 1959 and 1965. He is currently Professor at the Institut d'Architecture et Etudes Urbaines in Strasbourg, although he lives and works in New York and has an office in Paris. Pesce is known for his multi-disciplinary approach, and his work ranges from architecture to industrial design, exhibition design, drawing, sculpture, music, fashion and urban planning. He has worked for international companies such as Cassina, Italy; Knoll International, USA; and Vitra, Switzerland. Many of his works are in the permanent collections of major design museums, including the Metropolitan Museum of Art, New York; the Musée des Arts Décoratifs and the Centre Georges Pompidou, Paris; and the Musée des Arts Décoratifs, Montreal. For the Centennial of the Venice Biennale in June 1995, Pesce designed 10,000 one-off resin vases, and in 1996 a major retrospective of his work was held at the Centre Georges Pompidou. Major works include the "Organic Building", Osaka (1990–93), and the Chiat/Day office, New York; currently Pesce is working on the TBWA Chiat/Day extension in the same high-rise building, as well as a collection of affordable domestic objects distributed under the Fish Design label.

Pica & Sullivan Architects Ltd, 1036 South Alfred Street, Los Angeles, California 90035, USA

Pica & Sullivan is the architecture and interior design company of Joseph Pica and Maureen Sullivan. Pica studied at the University of Southern California School of Architecture. He has been involved in a variety of building types from commercial offices and hotels to institutional structures, medical and entertainment facilities. Prior to forming his partnership with Maureen Sullivan, he worked as Project Director at Arthur Erickson Architects, Senior Associate at Bretteville and Polyzoides, and Director of Design with Lee, Burkhart, Liu Inc. Sullivan also graduated from the University of Southern California School of Architecture. Before founding her own practice she worked for Levin and Associates as Senior Associate; she was responsible for many renovation schemes, most notably the award-winning restoration of the Wiltern Theater (1988), as well as the planning and design for the Pasadena Civic Center West development. Since 1989, she has held the position of Assistant Professor with the California State University at Long Beach and has recently received a grant to begin work on a series of books about architecture

for children. Sullivan is a member of the Los Angeles Conservancy. Pica and Sullivan now enjoys a considerable international reputation, with the partners each taking control of their areas of expertise. Pica has been involved in various leisure industry designs as well as the master planning and exterior design for the Broadway Elementary School, design guidelines for new construction of Twentieth-Century-Fox studios, and the design of the Virtual World Centers for Virtual World Entertainment worldwide. Sullivan is principal in charge of all projects in the historic Grand Central Market in Los Angeles, and is involved in tenant improvement and exterior renovation projects in the historic Bradbury Building.

Popp Planning and Development in Architectural and Town Planning Applications, Krummestrasse 58, Berlin 10627, Germany

Wolfram Popp is a self-taught architect who obtained a Diploma from the University of Stuttgart. In 1986 he was involved in the study of the relationship between new media and architecture and has since taught at the Technical University in Berlin and the Bauhaus University, Weimar. Important architectural projects include the Art Museum in Bonn (1984); a monument for Hanover (1985); social housing in Berlin (1985); a gallery building in a park in London's Docklands (1986); the Ethnology Museum in Frankfurt; public space projects in Berlin (1987–88); an exhibition gallery in Kassel (1989) and offices for Mediummulti, a multimedia co-operative in Berlin.

Rockwell Architecture, Planning and Design PC, 5 Union Square West, New York, NY 10003, USA

Rockwell Architecture is best known for its entertainment architecture and highly dramatic and spectacular interiors such as Nobu, Vong, Monkey Bar in New York, as well as nearly all the Planet Hollywood restaurants. The company is also concerned, however, with residential, retail, mixed-use and commercial projects. They are experts in the use of high-tech video technology, handmade objects and special effects. Clients include The Walt Disney Company; CBS; McDonalds, Caesar's World; and Sony Theatres. Projects currently at the design stage or under construction include the Official All Star Café in Times Square, New York, Disney's Creative Palate Restaurant, the CBS Retail Store on Broadway and an entertainment complex for Forest City Ratner with a floor space of 190,000 square feet on West 42nd Street. The Rockwell Group has received numerous major design awards and its work has been widely published. David Rockwell was born in 1956 in Chicago and moved to Guadalajara. He took a Bachelor's degree in architecture at the University of Syracuse and went on to study at the Architectural Association in London.

Richard Rogers Partnership, Thames Wharf, Rainville Road, London W6 9HA, UK

Richard Rogers founded his own practice with John Young, Marco Goldschmied and Mike Davies in 1977. Since then they have built a wide range of projects ranging from low-cost

industrial units to prestigious headquarters; from highly technical laboratories to landscape proposals; from cultural centres to office developments, and from airports to the restoration of historic monuments. Their most notable schemes include the Centre Georges Pompidou (1977), which has attracted more visitors than the Louvre and Eiffel Tower combined, and the Lloyds Building, London. Recent public commissions have included the European Court of Human Rights, Strasbourg, and the Law Courts in Bordeaux, and their work with historic buildings can be seen in the award-winning restoration and conversion of the old Billingsgate Fish Market in the City of London into a bankers' dealing room (1988). Other schemes in London include the Headquarters Building for Channel 4 Television and offices for Daiwa and Lloyds Register of Shipping; they are currently working on designs for Heathrow Airport's Terminal 5 and modifications for Terminal 1. The Partnership's interest in urban planning has recently won them the South Bank Centre Competition, a scheme that drew on experience gained in master planning such projects as the Potsdamer Platz, Berlin and the Lu Jia Zui business district in China. Richard Rogers received the Royal Gold Medal for Architecture from the Royal Institute of British Architects and was made Chevalier, L'Ordre National de la Legion d'Honneur in 1986. He was Chairman of the Tate Gallery (1986–89) and of the Building Experiences Trust (1989–94), and became a vice-chair of the Arts Council in 1994. He received a knighthood for services to architecture in the 1991 Birthday Honours List and was awarded the Ordre des Arts et des Lettres (1995).

RTKL UK Ltd, The Heals Building, 196 Tottenham Court Road, London W1P 9LD, UK

The London office of RTKL was opened in 1990 and now employs over 40 staff. Recently finished and current schemes include Fenix Park, Belgium; Centro Oberhausen, Germany; The Trocadero, London; Gaia Shopping, Oporto and Warner Bros Cinemas, Leicester, Dagenham, Leeds and Bolton, UK. The master company RTKL is an international architecture, planning and design firm involved in urban design, landscape architecture, interior design, engineering and renovation. It has projects in more than 45 countries, and offices in Europe, the Pacific and North America.

Schneider + Schumacher, Schlensenstrasse 17, 60327 Frankfurt, Germany

Schneider + Schumacher was created in 1988 by Till Schneider and Michael Schumacher, who both trained at the University of Kaiserslautern although Schneider finally gained his diploma from the Technische Hochschule in Darmstadt. Born in 1959 and 1957 respectively, they carried out postgraduate studies at the Staatliche Hochschule für Bildende Künste in Frankfurt under Peter Cook, following which Schneider worked independently for Eisele & Fritz in Darmstadt and Professor Robert Mürb in Karlsruhe. Schumacher moved to the UK, where he worked on a freelance basis for Sir Norman Foster before returning to Germany and joining the office of Braun &

Schlockermann in Frankfurt.

Stanton Williams, 10 Huguenot Place, Heneage Street, London E1 5LJ, UK

Stanton Williams was founded by Alan Stanton and Paul Williams in 1966. Stanton studied at the Architectural Association in London and at the University of California. He worked with Richard Rogers and Renzo Piano on the Centre Georges Pompidou from 1970 to 1977, and in collaboration with Mike Dowd designed an exhibition space in the Museum of Science and Industry at La Villette in Paris. Before this he worked for Foster Associates and as Partner in the architectural firm Chrysalis in Los Angeles. Paul Williams studied at Birmingham College of Art and later at the Yale Arts Center. He worked as Head of Design at the Victoria and Albert Museum and in private practice, where he was involved primarily in the design of exhibition spaces and installations, including shows at the Hayward Gallery, the Royal Academy of Arts, the refurbishment of the Introductory Galleries at Luton Hoo, and the Japanese Primary Gallery at the Victoria and Albert Museum. Major projects undertaken since the formation of the partnership include permanent and temporary exhibition galleries at the Design Museum (1989); offices and shops for Issey Miyake; Classic FM Studios (1992) and a 700-square-metre extension to the Ashmolean Museum in Oxford. They are currently working on a building to house two lecture theatres for Birkbeck College, London University; a Master Plan for the National Theatre in London, and the Millennium Seed Bank, which is a 5,000-square-metre building designed to store the Royal Botanic Garden's collection of seeds.

Steidle & Partner, Genter Strasse 13, 80805 Munich, Germany

Otto Steidle was born in Munich in 1943, and studied engineering at the Munich State Building College and architecture at the Munich Academy of Arts. In 1965, he founded the Muhr & Steidle architectural office, followed four years later by Steidle & Partner. He has taught at Kassel University and Berlin Technical University, and is Visiting Professor at the Massachusetts Institute of Technology and the Berlage School, Amsterdam. He is currently Vice-Chancellor of the Munich Academy of Fine Arts. Major projects include offices for Grüner & Jahr (1986–90); the University of Ulm (1988–92); and the development of Lehrter Strasse in Berlin (1991–94). Forthcoming projects are the Wacker Chemical Headquarters, Munich; housing in Potsdam; a shopping complex in Landshut; and a conference centre in Salzburg.

Robert A. M. Stern Architects, 211 West 61st Street, New York, NY 10023, USA

Robert A. M. Stern Architects was founded in the late 1960s. The practice is involved in architecture, landscape design and interior design, specializing in residential, commercial and institutional work in Europe, Asia and the USA. Its highly distinctive classic revivalism has won numerous prizes, including the National Honor Awards of the American Institute of Architects

in 1980, 1985, 1990 and 1991. Recently completed projects include the Ohrstrom Library, St Paul's School, Newhaven; the Norman Rockwell Museum, Stockbridge, Massachusetts; the Newport Bay Hotel and Cheyenne Hotel, USA; Euro Disney, Marne-La Vallée, France; the Center for Jewish Life, Princeton University; the Information Sciences Building at Stanford University, California; the Walt Disney Feature Animation Building, Burbank, California; and resort hotels in Japan. Robert Stern graduated from Columbia University in 1960 and from Yale in 1965. Today he is a Professor at the Graduate School of Architecture, Planning and Preservation at Columbia University and has lectured extensively in the USA and abroad. He is the author of several books, including *Modern Classicism* (1988). In 1976 and 1980 he was among the architects selected to represent the USA at the Venice Biennale. He serves on the board of directors of the Walt Disney Company, the Chicago Institute of Architecture and Urbanism, and the New York Architectural League.

Studio Thun, Via Appiani 9, Milan 20121, Italy

Matteo Thun was born in Bolzano, Italy, in 1952. He attended the Oskar Kokoschka Academy in Salzburg and graduated in architecture from the University of Florence. He worked for a period in Los Angeles, where he was involved in the aviation industry. On his return to Italy he founded Sottsass Associati with Ettore Sottsass, and also the Memphis Group where he stayed until 1984. At present, he deals mainly with industrial design, architecture, furnishings, corporate identity, graphics and packaging. He exhibits and lectures widely, both nationally and internationally, and his products have won numerous awards, including three Compasso d'Oro prizes in 1987 for *Mandelli 6*; in 1989 for a set of vases *Sherry Netherlands*, manufactured by Borovier and in 1991 for *Numeric Control*, again manufactured by Mandelli. He is a member of the jury for various design competitions. His works appear in the permanent collections of many leading art and design museums, including the Cooper-Hewitt Museum, New York, and the Victoria and Albert Museum, London. The artistic career and projects of Matteo Thun are documented in the monograph *Matteo Thun*, edited by Alex Buck and Matthias Vogt (1993).

Tibbatts Associates Limited, No. 1 St Paul's Square, Birmingham B3 1QU, UK

Tibbatts Associates are involved in designing specialist operations for the leisure and hospitality industry and work for corporate concerns, national and international operating companies and private entrepreneurial clients. They are also active in urban regeneration and have received commendations from the Secretary of State for their achievements. They are currently working on 1 million square feet of state-of-the-art technology buildings on reclaimed ex-contaminated land for one of the largest development corporations in the UK.

Von Gerkan, Marg & Partner, 139 Elbchausee, Hamburg, Germany

Von Gerkan, Marg & Partner is one of the most successful

architectural firms in Germany. Founder Meinhard von Gerkan was born in 1935 and studied in Berlin and Brunswick. In 1965, he began a collaboration with architect Volkwin Marg, and within the first year the team won seven first prizes in competitions, including one for the Berlin Tegel airport. The firm has been known as Von Gerkan, Marg & Partner since 1972, and has won over ninety national and international competitions, and received numerous other awards. In 1974, Meinhard von Gerkan became Professor at the Technical University of Brunswick. Important projects include airports in Moscow, Hanover, Stuttgart and Hamburg; the Convention Hall in Bielefeld; the Neue Messe in Leipzig; and Zürich-Insurance, Hamburg.

Jean-Michel Wilmotte, 68 rue du Faubourg Saint-Antoine, 75012 Paris, France

Jean-Michel Wilmotte was born in 1948 and studied at the Ecole Camondo before establishing Governor in 1975 in Paris to design interiors, furniture and lighting. In 1986 offices were opened in Nîmes and Tokyo. Wilmotte's work includes architecture and urban landscaping/street furniture. Major projects are the renovation of Nîmes town hall and museum; galleries and a bookshop at the Grand Louvre; Espace Kronenbourg, Paris; the Bunkamura Cultural Centre, Tokyo; the Musée des Beaux Arts, Bordeaux; first-floor galleries in the Richelieu Wing of the Grand Louvre, and the Institut International de la Mode, Marseilles.

Wingårdh Arkitektkontor AB, Kungsgaten 10A, 6Van, 411 19 Gothenburg, Sweden

Gert Wingårdh was born in Skövde, Sweden, in 1951 and moved to Gothenburg in 1961. He trained at the Chalmers Tekniska Högskolan, graduating in 1975 by which time he had already received a prize in a regional architectural competition for his design for a new church in Växjö. He worked for various architectural companies before forming his own studio in 1977; this went through different forms and amalgamation until becoming Wingårdh Arkitektkontor Ltd in 1992. Notable projects include the Villa Nilson; the Oij Ared Executive Country Club; the Hotel Scandic Crown and the Astra Hässle laboratories. Gert Wingårdh is currently a member of the Royal Academy of the Liberal Arts.

Yamashita Sekkei Inc., Omori Bellport Bldg A, 6-26-1 Minami-ohi, Shinagawa-ku, Tokyo 140, Japan

Yamashita Sekkei was founded in 1928 by Toshiro Yamashita Today it has branches in several cities within Japan and has also had offices in New York since 1988. Award-winning schemes include the Head Offices of Yasuda Insurance (1963); the Sendai Municipality Office Building (1967); the Kasumigaseki Building (1969); the NHK Broadcasting Centre (1974); the Shirayur Women's College Library (1984); the Fujitsu Kawasaki Technology Centre (1990) and the Yokohama Learning Centre of Nomura (1992).

1 THE MULTIMEDIA INDUSTRY

Channel 4 Television Company Headquarters, London, UK

Architect and interior design: Richard Rogers Headquarters. Project team: Laurie Abbott; Yasmin Al-Ani; Oliver Collignon; Mark Collins; Helen Brunskill; Mark Darbon; Mike Davies; Jane Donnelly; Florian Fischötter; Marco Goldschmied; Philip Gumuchdjian; Jackie Hands; Bjork Haraldsdottir; Stig Larsen; Carmel Lewin; Stephen Light; Avtar Lotay; John Lowe; Steve Martin; Andrew Morris; Elizabeth Parr; Louise Pritchard; Kim Quazi; Richard Rogers; Daniel Sibert; Stephen Spence; Kinna Stallard; Graham Stirk; Yuli Toh; Alec Vassiliades; Martin White; Adrian Williams; Megan Williams; John Young. Client: Channel 4 Television Company. Main contractor: Bovis Construction Ltd. Structural engineers: Ove Arup & Partners. Traffic engineers: Ove Arup & Partners. M&E engineers: YRME. Quantity surveyors: The Wheeler Group Consultancy. Acoustic consultants: Sandy Brown Associates. Planners: Westminster City Council. Rights of light consultants: McBains Building Surveyors. Ergonomics consultant: Satherley Design. Landscape: Branch Landscape Associates; Warrington Fire Research Consultants; Studio Design Partnership; Maxtel Telecommunications. Concrete: R. O'Rourke & Son Ltd. Steelwork: Westbury Tubular Structures plc. Sundry Metalwork: W & R Leggott Ltd. Cladding: Permasteelisa; Colomban Massimo; Johnny Foo; Fiancarlo Iovino. Weathering: Coverite Ltd. Suspended ceiling: Barrett Ceilings Ltd. Office partitions: Permasteelisa. Raised floor: Hewetson Floors Ltd. Studio floor finish: Seamless Surfaces. Floor finishes: A1 Flooring Ltd. Stonework: Grants of Shoreditch; Doors: Bolton Brady. Roller shutter: Amber Industrial Doors Ltd. Decorations: Ian Williams Ltd. Fabric wall covering: IAC Ltd. Fit Out: Faithdean Ltd. Acoustics: IAC Ltd. Kitchen equipment: Hallmark; Cuisine Food Services. Furniture and fittings: Aram Design. Window blinds: Technical Blinds. Window cleaning equipment: Kobi Cradles Ltd. Mechanical: Andrew Weatherfoil Ltd. Electrical: T. Clarke Ltd. Lift: Otis.

Disney Feature Animation Building, Burbank, California, USA

Architect and interior design: Robert A. M. Stern Architects. Project team/architecture: Barry Rice, Paul Whalen (Architects-in-Charge); Michael Jones; Dan Lobitz; Geoffrey Mouen; Rosamund Young. Project team/interior design: Alex Lamis, Barry Rice (Architects-in-Charge); Adam Anuszkiewicz; Valerie Hughes; Jane Whitford. Client: Disney Development Company. Architect of Record: Morris Architects. General contractor: McCarthy Construction. Structural engineers: De Simone Chaplin and Dobryn Consulting Engineers PC. MEP: Cosentini Associates. Civil engineers: Psomas Associates. Geotechnical: Law/Crandell Inc. Lighting design: Imero Fiorentino Associates, Inc.; Cosentini Lighting Design. Acoustic engineers: Charles M. Salter Associates, Inc. Screening room consultants: Lucas Film Ltd. Architectural signage/graphic design: Beck & Graboski Design Office. Landscape: SWA Group. Cost and scheduling: CBA Ltd. Elevator consultants: John A. Van Deusen & Associates Inc.

CLM/BBDO, Paris, France

Architect and interior design: Jean Nouvel et Associé. Project Architects: Marie-Hélène Baldran (Architects); E. Manchon; John Thornhill (Assistant Architect); Valérie Véron-Durand (CAD design); Vincent Hubert; James Noble; Alan Mac (design); Sabine Rosant (graphic design). Client: CLM/BBDO. Main contractors: JMS; C.J.2.B. Engineers: INTER G (electricity); SBX (heating); Technology; DEGW (Space planning); EA (engineering control). Landscape architect: Ingénieurs et Paysages; Via Park; Algaflex; Tout Rois. Consultants: Cotect Maitrise d'Oeuvre de Réalisation; Gary Glaser; Alain Bony. Quantity surveyor: Delporte Hautmont. False floor: Polytravaux; Ouvrard. Façade and grilles: Batex. Sliding doors: Besam. Woodwork: Fortier; Douaud. Mirrors: Saprover. Office partitions: Orion. Glass partitions: Souchier. False ceilings: Artemis. Interior paintwork/parquet: Bechet. Exterior paintwork: Eppi. Communal structures/electricty: Santerne. Ventilation: Foret. Plumbing: SGT. Space planning and furniture: Unifor. Waterproofing: SMAC Acierôd. Blinds: Arbeca. Tiles: Canto. Framework structure: Maurizi. False ceiling: Vidili.

Mediummulti (Pixelpark), Berlin, Germany

Architect: Dipl. Ing. Wolfram Popp. Client: Pixelpark Multimediagesellschaften mbH. Consulting engineer: Dipl. Ing. Johann Schneider. Joinery: Fritz Funk.

TBWA Chiat/Day Inc. Offices, New York, USA

Interior design: Gaetano Pesce/Pesce Ltd. Project team: Gaetano Pesce (Principal and Design); Kent Hikida (Project Architect); Olafur Thordarson V.P.; Patrick Rannou Douglas Bergert, Lisa Hill, Denise Ha (Architectural Team); Michael Schinelli; Zingg Avi Cohen; Darin Johnstone; Leonid Yentus; Joseph Sabel; Michael Whitney; Jason Tillman. Client: TBWA Chiat/Day Inc. Advertising. Contractors: Tony Pugliese/Paintcraft (custom interior painting and fabric wall finishes); Ruvolo & Di Maria (custom wooden tables); Metrospace (millwork); CTI (walls and ceilings); Versailles (upholstery); Metalforms and Kraman (metal fabrications); Penguin (A/C mechanical); Alex Manuelle; Fosdick/Bills. Consultants: JB&B (electrical engineering); Thorton Tomasetti (structural engineering); A&H (architectural); Siemens Rolm (telephone systems); Tri-Met. (shop drawings).

SMA Video Inc, New York, USA

Architect and interior design: Anderson/Schwartz Architects. Project team: Ross Anderson (Partner-in-charge); Stephen O'Dell (Project Architect); Aaron Bently; M.J. Sagan; Caroline Otto; Paul Cali. Client: SMA Video Inc. Main contractor: Clark Construction. Mechanical engineer: I.P. Group. Acoustical engineers: Shen Milson & Wilkie, Inc. Mechanical sub-contractor: Hennick-Lane Inc. Electrical sub-contractor: JBC Electrical Construction Inc. Drywall sub-contractor: Ronsco, Inc. Millwork and finishes: Primo Construction. Steel fabrication: Face Architecture & Fabrication. Console fabrication: Forecast; Ferra. Lighting: Killark (Hubbel Div.); Stonco Lighting Services Inc.; Litetrom Inc.; Times Square Lighting; Belfer Lighting;

Reggiani; Halo; Metalux Inc.; Adjusco Task Lights; Canyon Lights. Furniture: Eames custom designed and fabricated. Fabrics: Calvin Fabrics; Rogers & Goffigon Ltd. Flooring: Forbo Inc. Marmoleum; CTEC; American Olean and United Ceramic (ceramic tiles); Monteray Carpet.

Thomson Consumer Electronics Administration Building (Americas Headquarters), Indianapolis, Indiana, USA

Architect and interior design: Michael Graves Architect. Project team: Michael Graves (Design Principal); Gary Lapera (Senior Associate-in-Charge); Wendy Bradford (interior design). Client: Thomson Consumer Electronics. Associate architect: Haldeman, Powell, Johns Architects. Main contractor: Browning Construction Inc. Sub-contractor: Concrete Technology Inc. Lighting consultant: Maggie Giusto. Furniture and fittings: Business Furniture Corp. Skylights: Fischer Skylights. Suppliers: Otis Elevators; Concrete Tech, Inc.; Architect Glass & Metal; Diener Brick; L. M. Scofield Company (precast pigment).

Telecom Center, Tokyo, Japan

Architect: Nissoken/HOK joint venture. Nissoken project team: Junkichi Kurahashi (Principal Designer); Hideaki Ota (Project Manager/Designer); Satoshi Osozaki (Field Supervisor). HOK project team: Gyo Obata (Principal Designer); Ernest Cirangle (Project Designer); Takehiko Watanabe; Carol Mancke (Field Supervisors). Client: Tokyo Teleport Center Inc. Collaborator: Moyoko Ishii (lighting). Contractors: Taisei; Kajima; Tokyu; Obayashi; Schal Bovis; Tokai Kogyo; Seibu; Katamura (west block); Kandenko; Toenec; Sumitomo; Denkosha; Tomiyo Denki (electrical); Taikisha; Hibiya Sogo; Yamato; Nissen-Nissin; Takamura Sogo (mechanical).

VG-Huset, Oslo, Norway

Architect: Lund & Slaatto Arkitekter AS. Client: Verdens Gang (VG) Oslo. Interior design: ArkiForum AS. Main contractor: Eeg-Henriksen Bygg AS. Mechanical and electrical engineers: Nilsen & Borge AS. HVAC engineers: Erichsen & Horgen AS. Landscape architect: Landskapsarkitekter AS. Suppliers: Hole Glass AS (roof and façades in glass and aluminium); Naturstein AS (stones in façades, floors and staircases).

Leo Burnett Advertising Headquarters, London, UK

Architect: YRM/Stanton Williams. Project team: Alan Farlie; Russell Gilchrist; Rebekah Gomez; Richard Griffin; Frank Heaversdege; Michael Langley; Simon McCormack; Ivan Margolius; Peter Murray; Robin Nicholson; Alan Stanton; Gary Turnbill; Ben Vickery; James Wells; Paul Williams. Client: Glenlake Limited. Main contractor: Wimpey Construction. Project manager: E.C. Harris. Structural engineers: YRM/Anthony Hunt Associates. Service engineers: YRM Engineers. Planning consultants: Town Planning Consultants. Quantity surveyors. Leonard Stace Partnership. Steelwork: Littlehampton Welding. Main cladding: Felix UK; Stone Cladding International. Atrium and entrance screen glazing:

Pilkington. Replacement windows: Mellowes Archital; Shopfronts: Felix UK. Restoration/cleaning of terracotta: London Stone; Bingdon Builders. Masonry, brickwork, block-work: Tiltlynn. Roofing: BFR. Lifts and escalators: Schindler. M&E, Health and Drainage: Matthew Hall. Plastering: Whiteways Contractors. Raised floors: Hewetson. Ceilings: SAS; Astec. Doors, joinery: Raphael Construction. Metal doors and shutters: Henderson Industrial. Doors, ironmongery: Elementar. Internal doors: NT Shapland & Petter. Lighting: Elementer; Erco, Philips. Stone: Cumbria Stone Quarries. Metalwork: Robinson Metalwork. Wall finishes: Peruchetti. Floor finishes: Seamless Surfaces; Mactail. Decorations and coatings: Daniels Decorations. Interior design fit-out: Fletcher Priest. Contractor: Constructive Interiors. Acoustics: Arup Associates. Fit-out suppliers: Audio Visual: AVE Group. Glass screens (office fronts), tea-coffee points, meeting room cabinets, metal panels: Hills of Shoeburyness. Partitions: HL Smith Construction (Optima 97). Private magic glass: St. Gobain; Pollards Fyrespan. Movable partitions: Huppe Form; Unilock. Café and bar fittings: Arden & Hodges; HNB Contracts. Patinated metal bar counter: Verdigris. Dining room fittings: HNB; Arden & Hodges. Meeting room polished plaster: Armouralia. Blinds: Colt International. Carpet: Esco (UK). Lighting: Elementar Lighting. Small works: D&M Kain. BMS: Staefa Control Systems. Cladding: Felix Glass. Storage: Waiko UK. Desking: WII Group. Security: BDI Security. Doors: FR Shadbolt. Signage: Graphex; Town & Country Signs. Carpet fitter: Britefox. Roof terrace: Farrugia. Planting: Indoor Garden Design.

2 ADVANCED OFFICE ENVIRONMENTS

Head Office National Nederlanden and ING Bank, Budapest, Hungary

Architect and interior design: EEA Erick van Egeraat Associated Architects. Project team : Erick van Egeraat; Tibor Gall (Project Architects); Maartje Lammers (Assistant Architect); Astrid Huwald; Gabor Kruppa; Janos Tiba; Stephen Moylan; Williams Richards; Ineke Dubbeldam; Ard Buijsen; Miranda Nieboer; Harry Boxelaar; Axel Koschany; Tamra Klassen. Client: National-Nederlanden Hungary Ltd; ING Bank Budapest; ING Real Estate. Main contractor: CFE Hungary Epitoipara Kft. Management services: Pro Plan Kft. Quantity surveyor: Munk Dunstones Associates. Structrual consultant: ABT Adviesburo voor Boutwtechniek bv. Mechanical and electrical consultant: Ketel Raadgevend Ingenieurs bv. Glass construction: Permasteelisa, Conegliano. Interior contractors: Van Gils projekten bv.; Patella; Desseaux; Ketel projektservice. Lifts: Otis Hungary. Mechanical services: Air & Chaleur. Electrical services: VIV Siemens. Models: Henk Bouwer.

Banco Santander Headquarters, Madrid, Spain

Architect and interior design: Prof Hans Hollein Architect. Project team: Hans Hollein (Design Principal); Ulf Kotz (Project Architect); Klaus Matauschek; Sina Baniahmad; Richard Goodstein; Russel Katz; Kevin Mulcahy; Jimena Robles. Client:

Banco Santander. Client's representatives: Javier de Lahidalga; Gonzalo Echenique (building department, Madrid); Alfonso Millanes (resident architect, Madrid). Collaborator: Manue Ayllon Campillo of Jaime Ferrer Sarroca Arquitectos. General contractor: Formento de Construcciones y Contratos SA. Lighting consultant: Lichtdesign Ingenieurges MbH.

Banque de Luxembourg, Luxembourg

Architect and interior design: Arquitectonica International Corporation. Project team: Bernardo Fort-Brescia (Principal); Laurinda Spear (Principal), Nicolas de Rochfort. Client: Banque de Luxembourg. Local Associate Architect: Bureaux d'Architecture Fiorenzo Cavallini. Main contractor: CDC-Compagnie de Construction. Engineering: Groupe Ingenierie Alsace; Elie Mokbel (Geotechnical Engineer); Gilles Voinchet (Civil Engineer); Christian Siegwald (Structural Engineer); Mr Daniel Schuester (Mechanical/plumbing Engineer); Hubert Jund (Electrical & Security, Life, Safety Engineer). HVAC consulting engineer: Bureau d'Etudes Jean Schmit. Project co-ordination and structural engineer: Secolux. Lighting: Plasticien Eclaragiste. Furniture and fittings: Jean-Michel Wilmotte. Flooring: Arquitectonica; Jean-Michel Wilmotte. Walls, ceilings, partitions: Arquitectonica. Façades consultant: Albrecht Memmert. Acoustical consultant: Werner Genest und Partner. Audio-visual consultant: Auvitec.

Isar Büro Park, Hallbergmoos, Munich, Germany

Architect and interior design: Maki and Associates in collaboration with Architekten Schmidt-Schicketanz und Partner GmbH. Project team, Maki and Associates: Fumihiko Maki (Principal); Kei Mizui; Toshio Hachiya, Gary Kamemoto; Akiki Ikeda; Norio Yokota; Lawrence Mattot; Ulrike Liebel; Kunio Watanabe; Haruo Ohashi. Project team, Schmidt-Schicketanz und Partner: Otto Bertermann; Eberhard Steinert; Bettina Hamann; Gabi Selgrath; Martin Pitzke; Eva Neumeyer; Renate Pfanzelt; Omar Guebel; Sigrid Kunzmann; Jürgen Mrosko; Gebhard Weiberhorn; Makoto Mizushima. Client: Deutsche Grundbesitz – Investmentgesellschaft mbH. Main contractor: Arbeitsgemeinschaft Isar Büro Park Hallbergmoos. Sub-contractors: Mannesmann Anlagenbau AG (HVAC); Rheinelektra AG (electrical company); Beer Spezial-Stahlbau (steel construction); R & M Ritter Ingenieufasaden GmbH (glass façade and glass roof). Structural engineer: Sohmmitt-Stump & Frühauf. HVAC and mechanical: Energie System Plannungs GmbH. Electrical engineering and lighting: Ingenieurbüro Barth & Hildebrand. Glass façade and roof: Ingenieurbüro Fuchs. Landscaping: Sasaki Environment Design Office Co. Ltd; Cordes & Partner Projektgesellschaft mbH. Building physics, noise protection: Müller BBM GmbH. Lighting: Zerbetto; Litec; Leymann; Winterhager; Bega; Louis Poulsen; Hoffmeister. Flooring: George Nahar (office carpets); Villeroy & Boch (bathroom "Pro Architectura" tiles); Freudenberg (rubber "Normanebt 925" tiles). Office furniture: "Mehes plus" by Ahrend. Self-cooling ceilings: ABB Fläkt. Textiles: M & V ("Heliostore" blinds); Ivera "Tabella Flamm Plus" (shades under glass roof). Metal roof: Alcan ("Falzonal" aluminium sheets).

NTT Shinjuku Headquarters Building, Tokyo, Japan

Architect and interior design: Cesar Pelli & Associates. Project team: Cesar Pelli (Design Principal); Fred Clarke (Project Principal); Jun Mitsui; Gregg Jones; David Chen (Design Team Leaders); Kevin Burke; Karen Koenig; Hirotaka Otsuji; Masami Yonasawa; Douglas McIntosh; Roger Schickedantz; Robert Espejo; Ruth Bennett; Scott Aquilina. Client: Nippon Telegraph and Telephone Corporation. Architect of Record: Yamashita Sekkei, Rintaro Murata (Architect-in-Charge); Katsihiko Oozeki; Eiichi Takahashi; Masahiro Katsume; Masayoshi Tsumoto; Kouji Watanabe; Mazazumi Yoshida; Kouji Kobori. Main contractors: JV; Taisei Corporation; Kajima Corporation; Overseas Bechtel Inc.; Takenaka Corporation; Fujita Corporation; Hazama Corporation. Engineers: Yamashita Sekkei Inc. (structural, mechanical, electrical, value); Architectural Lighting: H. M. Brandston & Partners Inc. Landscape: Balmori Associates; Some Landscape Planning Co. Ltd. Electrical work: JV; Kinden Corporation; Toko Electrical Construction Co. Ltd; Sanyo Engineering and Construction Inc.; Oki Electric Installation Co. Ltd. Air-conditioning and plumbing: JV; Takasago Thermal Engineering Co. Ltd; Sanken Setsubi Kogyo Co. Ltd; Toyonetsu Kogyo Kabushikigaishaya; Dai-den Co. Ltd, Sankyo Air Conditioning Co. Ltd. Elevator: Hitachi Ltd. Aluminium curtain wall: Tostem Corporation and Kawneer, Nihon Kentetsu Co. Ltd and Benson Co. Ltd; Nikkei Urban Build Co. Ltd and Wansan Metals Corporation. Heat reflecting glass: Guardian Industries; Asahi Glass Company. Roof: Vetter Stone Ltd.; Burlington Slate Ltd. Floor tiles: Milliken Carpet.

SUVA, Basle, Switzerland

Architect: Herzog & de Meuron. Project team: Astrid Poisard; Kurt Lazzarini; Dieter Gysin, Michelle Erbsland; Ursula Kaspar; Ansgar Adamczyk; Christoph Schlemmer; Christoph Steiger; Pascale Guignard; Peter Kaufmann; Rina Plangger; Robert Hösl; Sämi Häusermann; Stefan Marbach. Client: Schweizerische Unfallversicherungsanstalt. Project management: Paul Ernst. Façade engineering and co-ordination: Schmidtin AG; A. Müller . Technical co-ordination: W. Widmann. Heating and ventilation: W. Waldhuaser AG. Sanitation: Bogenschutz AG. Surveyor: Gysin & Ehrsan AG. Structural engineer: Ingenieurgemeinschaft A. Zachmann. Auditorium engineer: Confa AG. Landscaping: Stöckli, Kienast & Koeppel.

Crédit Lyonnais Tower, Lille, France

Architect: Atelier Christian de Portzamparc. Project team: Christian de Portzamparc; François Barberot; Bruno Barbot; Bertrand Beau; Bruno Durbecq; Paul Guilleminot; Benoit Juret; Marie-Elizabeth Nicoleau; Etienna Pierrès; Oliver Souquet. Client: Ferinel Industries – Groupe George V, Crédit Lyonnais. Site architect: Euralille; Rem Koolhaas. Main contractor: Caroni – Groupe CBC. Project control: SOCOTEC. Structural engineer: S.E.E.R. Façade: C.E.E.F. Heating and ventilation: C.G.C. Paintwork, ceilings and floors: Cabre. Partitions: Carnoy/ Entreprise Sorbati. Glazing: Daver. Stonework: Jean Luc Denis. False ceilings and metalwork: Dussart.

Plumbing: Huet/Ferroile. Security: Maurizi. Woodwork: MG/Metranor. Lifts: Otis.

Inland Revenue, Nottingham, UK

Architects: Michael Hopkins & Partners. Project team: Sir Michael Hopkins; Ian Sharratt; Peter Romaniuk; Peter Cartwright. Client: Inland Revenue. Main contractor: Laing Management. Engineers: Ove Arup & Partners. Quantity surveyors: Turner & Townsend. Acoustic consultants: Arup Acoustics.

Zenrosai Computer Centre, Tokyo, Japan

Architect and interior design: Dai'ichi-Kobo Associates. Project team: Tei'ichi Takahashi; Shigeru Fuse; Midori Otaki; Sadao Kobayashi; Masaru Ihara; Koichi Kikuchi. Main contractor: Taipei Corporation. Sub-contractor: Takasago Thermal Engineering Corporation. Structural engineer: Kozo-Keikaku Engineering Inc. Mechanical and electrical engineer: Planning and Air Conditioning Consultant Co. Ltd.

3 HYBRID CONSTRUCTIONS

Energie-Forum-Innovation, EHR Communication and Technology Centre, Bad Oeynhausen, Germany

Architect: Frank O. Gehry & Associates, Inc. Project team: Frank O. Gehry (Design Pincipal); Jim Glymph (Project Principal); Randall Stout (Project Architect and designer); Vince Snyder; Michael Maltzan (Project designers); Tomaso Bradshaw; Jonathan Davis; Matthias Seufert; Todd Spiegel; Hiroshi Tokumaru; Laurence Tighe; Tim Williams. Client: Elektizistätswerk Minden-Ravensberg GmbH. Associate Architect: EMR; Hartwig Rullkötter, AKNW. Structural engineer: John A. Martin (design); Dipl. Ing. Albert Grage (executive). Mechanical engineer: Ingenieubüro G, Reschke. Electrical engineer: Ingenieubüro R. Ruttenkroger. Lighting consultant: LAM Partners Inc. Lighting: Zumtobel Staff. Landscape design: Nancy Power & Associates. Exhibition design "Energy Forum Innovation": Hodgetts & Fung. Graphic design: Bruce Mau Design Inc.

Astra Hässle Research Centre, Gothenburg, Sweden

Architect, interior, laboratory and landscape design: Wingårdh Arkitektkontor AB. Project team: Anna Karin Andersson; Ulrika Bergström, Inger Borberg; Ake Boustedt; Magnus Börjeson; Anneli Carlsson; Johan Casselbrant; Claude Christensson; Dav Danielsson; Stefan Dallendorfer; Ulrike Davidson; Björn Dufva; Jonas Edblad; Torbjörn Edgren; Pär Eliasson; Pal Eriksson; Fredrik Gullberg; Lennart Gullberg; Foued Hajjam; Choukri Halila; Magnus Kardborn; Emma Kaudern; Vera Kniehova; Vanja Knocke; Jerry Kopare; Carina Lind; Patrik Nilson; Johan Norén; Thomas Ocklund; Urban Pihl; Jens Ragnarsson; Poul Erik Sörensen; Sören Steffensen; Ulf Thorbjörnsson; Raymond Tollbom. Client: Astra Hässle AB. Main contractors: Skanska; Siab; NCC; Platzer. Project management: Projsam AB. Structural engineer: Flygfältsbyran AB. Mechanical engineer: Bo Lönner AB; Andersson & Hultmark AB. Electrical engineer:

KM Elteknik AB. Acoustical engineer: Akustikforum AB. Lighting: Zumtobel Staff; Erco. Furniture: EFG (offices); Fritz Hansen, Matshon International (canteen). Laboratory fittings: Ninolab. Stone flooring: Olandssten. Gypsum walls: Gyproc.

Stadhus (City Hall and Central Library), The Hague, The Netherlands

Architect and interior design: Richard Meier & Partners, Architects. Project team: Richard Meier; Thomas Phifer; Gunter Standke (Project Design); Rijk Rietveld (Project Architect); Diederik Fokkema (Project Architect); Francisco Bielsa; Peter Bochek; John Bosch; Patricia Bosch Melendez; Paul Cha; Eric Cobb; Adam Cohen; Susan Davis McCarter; Hans van de Eijk; Kenneth Frampton; Stephen Harris; Gordon Hasslett; Raphael Justewicz; Gerard Kruunenberg; John Locke; Richard Manna; David Martin; Siobhan McInerney; Brian Messana; Marc Nelen; Alex Nussbaumer; Ana O'Brian; Hans Peter Petri; Hans Put; Greg Reaves; Marc Rosenbaum; Madelaine Sanchez; David Shultis. Client: City of The Hague. Structural engineer: Grabowsky & Poort. Mechanical and electrical engineer: BVS. Building physics: Peutzx & Associates. Landscape architects: Joan Busquets; Alle Hosper; De Kern Gezond.

Neue Messe, Leipzig, Germany

Architect: Von Gerkan, Marg und Partner. Project team: Prof. Volwin Marg (Project Director); Hubert Nienhoff; Kemal Akay (Project Manager); Beata Sturm; Christiane Hasskamp; Monika Scharrer; Veronika Kruch (east entrance); Nyna Bergfeld, Gabriele Köhn; Jutta Hartmann-Pohl (west entrance); Björn Bergfeld; Wolfgang Balbach; Suzanne Bern; Christina Harenberg; Almut Schlüter; Miriam Danke; Fulvio Melle; Klaus Courmont (exhibition halls); Armin Wittershagen; Uwe Friedrich; Annette Kersig; Robert Stüer; Jane Schmahl (pavilion restaurants); Ulrich Weigel; Gisbert v. Stühl-pnagel; Bernd Gossmann; Yasmin Balbach; Jochen Köhn; Michael Pohl; Aristide Hamann; Birgit Rith; Tom Naujack (congress centre); Christian Hoffmann; Hubert Hirsch; Dirk Kahlig; Elisabeth Menne; Clemens Dost; Ben Dieckmann; Fernanda Barbato; Monika Kaesler; Thomas Behr (administration building); Angelika Juppian; Petra Kauschus; Heike Bteuler (open-air utilities); Dieter Rösinger; Ursula Köper; Annette Löber; Verena von der Brincken; Wieland Freudiger (interior fittings and furniture); Franz Lensing; Marco Bartusch (metal construction, escalators, lifts and locksmith work); Reinhold Weiten; Hubercus v. Dallwitz (technical co-ordination and scheduling). Jochen Köhn, Robert Stüer (computer services); Ines Buchin; Annett Kretzler (administrative support) Leitung, Rolf Niedballa; Uwe Grahl; Hans-Peter Bentike; Andreas Ebner; Peter Krüger; Roland Lauer; Kerstin Mahler (Bill of quantity). Client: Leipziger Messegesellschaft MbH. Project management: IRW Ingenieurbüro Rauch und Wiese. Structural engineer: of steel–glass hall: gmp in co-operation with Ian Ritchie Architects. Civil Engineering: Obermeyer Albis-Bauplan; RWTH; Institut für Stadtplanung. Information Systems: Atelier Mac Kneissel. Façade consultant: PBI, Klaus Glass; Ing-Büro Wronn. Natural stone consultant: Ing-Büro Pinck. Technical systems:

HL-Technik; Ebert-Ingenieure. Structural design: Ing-Büro Polonyi & Partner; Ing-Büro H. Haringer. Insulation: Von Rekowski-Wolff. Acoustics: Akustik-Ing-Büro Moll, Ing-Büro Knothe. Shell and steel construction: Wayss & Freytag AG; Stahlbau Mauen GmbH (exhibition hall); Mero Raumstruktur GmbH; Glasbau Seele GmbH (glass hall); ARGE Messcturm, Stock GmbH; Stahlbau Illingen GmbH (construction tower); Techno-Metall GmbH; ARGE Seele/Friess (administration centre and congress centre). Façade construction exhibition hall: Fassadensysteme; Kulkwitz; Koldt GmbH. Façade glazing and sun-protection systems: Rheinhold & Mahla GmbH, Leipzig. Support free steel stairs: Hark GmbH & Co. KG. Railings of galleries: ARGE Schultz/Dahme; Metallbau Gayger. Metal and glass door structures: Breitenbach GmbH. Movable partition walls: Hüppe Form GmbH. Panorama lifts: Tepper-Aufzüge GmbH& Co. KG. Natural stone cladding: Kiefer-Reul-Teich GmbH. Concrete ashlar construction/flooring materials: Betonsteinwerk Uetze GmbH. Steel constructions: Arnold GmbH; Friedricksdorf/Ts Metall und Werkzeugbau GmbH. Landscaping: Wehberg; Schmidtke. Mature trees: Bruns-Pflanzen Export; Lorenz von Ehren. Furniture: Kayenburg Linear Einrichtung. Carpentry and interior fittings: Lindner AG; Ohning Innenausbau GmbH; Stöppler Innenausbau – Möbel Anfertigung; VHB Vereinigte Holzbau-berriebe GmbH & Co.

Science Park, Gelsenkirchen, Germany

Architects: Kiessler & Partner. Project team: Uwe Kiessler; Hermann Schultz; Vera Ilic; Stefanie Reithwiesner; Ursula Baptista; Thomas Brilling; Konstanze Elbel; Andreas Gierer; Klaus Jantschek; Achim Jürke; Markus Link; Klaus Löhnert; Christoph Mayr; Andreas Plesske. Client: Wissenschaftspark and Technologiezentrum Rheinelbe Gelsenkirchen Vermîgensgellschaft mbh. Project management: Norbert Muhlak. Structural engineer: Sailer & Stepan. Heating, ventilation and sanitation: Ingenieurbüro Trumpp. Electrical engineer: Planungsgemeinschaft Riemhofer/Zerull. Landscaping: Planungsbüro Drecker. Energy source consultant: Fraunhofer Institut für Solare Energiesysteme. Solar panels: Flachglas-Solartechnik GmbH. Façade consultant: Institut Schaupp. Office façades: Gebr. Schneider Fensterfabrik. Roof: Fa. Wewers GmbH. Tiling: Fa. H. Linnr. Floor coverings: Fa. Häcker.

Hôtel du Département, Des Bouches-du-Rhône, Marseilles, France

Architect: Alsop & Störmer. Project team: William Alsop; Francis Graves; Stephen Pimbley (directors); Jonathan Adams; James Allen; Sonia Andrade; Peter Angrave; Hilary Bagley; Russell Bagley; Stephan Biller; Florence Bobin; Pierre-André Bonnet; James Brearley; Joanne Burnham; Xavier d'Alenáon; Jason Dickinson; Sybil Diot-Lamige; Robert Evans; Roger Farrow; Colin Foster; Cristina Garcia Borja Goyarrola; Ivan Green; Astrid Huwald; Stephen James; John Kember; David Knill-Samuel; Nigel Lusty; Harvey Male; Paul Matthews; Roger Minost; Philippe Moinard; Suzy Murdock; Simon North; Sophie Palmer; Victoria Perry; Emmanuelle Poggi; Sanya Polescuk; Geoffrey Powis; John Prevc; Matthew Priestman; Stuart Rand-Bell;

Christian Richard; Anne Schmilinsky; Diana Stiles; Peter Strudwick; Gary Taylor; George Tsoutsos; Nick Van Oosten; Laurence York Moore; Petra Wesseler. Interior design: Alsop & Störmer; Ecart. Project team: Andrée Putman; Gérard Borgniet; Gilles Leborgne; Elliot Barnes; Marion Guidoni; Rovre, Bové. Client: Conseil Général des Bouches-du-Rhône. Consulting engineers: Ove Arup & Partners. Engineering sub-consultant: O.T.H. Méditerranée. Quantity surveyor: Hanscomb Ltd. Concrete structure: MCB/CBC. Cladding: Cabrol. Mechanical contractor: Albouy/AIC/TNEE. Electrical contractor: Cegelec. Lifts: Otis Elevator Co. Woodwork: Delta Menuiseries. Decoration: Bareau. Flooring and walls: Gambini. Paintwork and mirrors: Cantereil. Signage: Lettre & Lumière. False ceiling: Wanner Isofi. Lighting: Concord.

Compass Centre (British Airways Centre for Combined Operations), Heathrow Airport, UK

Architect: Nicholas Grimshaw & Partners. Project team: Stefan Camenind; Penny Collins; Robert Elliston; Rowena Fuller; Nicholas Brimshaw; Andrew Hall; Julian King; Rosemary Latter; Jonathan Leah; John Lee; John Martin; Liz Parr; David Portman; David Radford; Martin Wood. Client: Lynton plc for Heathrow Airport Ltd. Interior design: Davies Baron/Aukett. Construction management: Bovis Construction. Quantity surveyor: David Langdon & Everest. Structural engineer: YRM/Anthony Hunt Associates. Services engineer: J. Roger Preston & Partners. Acoustic consultant: Ian Findell & Associates. Radar consultant: Dowty Signature Management. External lighting consultant: Equation.

SSCT/System Solution Centre Tochigi, Utsunomiya, Japan

Architect and interior design: Architect 5 Partnership. Project team: Matsuoka Takeo; Junichi Kawamura; Hidetsugu Horikoshi; Hirotaka Kidosaki. Client: System Solution Centre Tochigi Inc. Collaborators: Ryozo Umezawa (structural engineer); Inuzuka (engineering consultants). Main contractor: Watanabe General Construction. Sub-contractor: Shinryo-Reinetsu Co. Furniture consultant: Ilya Corporation; Kandenko.

Research Institute of Innovative Technology for the Earth (RITE) Headquarters Building, Keihanna, Japan

Architect: Nikken Sekkei Ltd. Client: Research Institute of Innovative Technology for the Earth. Main contractor: Obayashi Corporation. Sub-contractors: Taisei Corporation; Takenaka Corporation; Kajima Corporation; Shimizu Corporation. Electrical work: Kinden Corporation. Air conditioning and plumbing: Taaikisha Ltd. Elevators: Hitachi Elevator Ltd.

Telefónica de España, Madrid, Spain

Architect: Francisco José Larrucea. Client: Telefónica de España SA. Collaborators: Larrucea y Colaboradores SL. Main contractor: Cubiertas M.Z.O.V. Contractors: Abengoa SA; Isolux Wat SA; Sintel.

Customers' Center for Systems Integration Motorola Inc., Schaumburg, Illinois, USA

Architect and interior design: Holabord & Root. Project team: Gerald Horn (Partner-in-Charge); Tom Meyer (Project Manager); Tod Desmarais (Project Designer); Khatija Hashmy (Project Architect); Patricia Sicha (interior design). Client: Motorola Inc. General contractor: Rudolph V. Schuh Co. Wallcovering: Bernhardt Textiles; DesignTex; Deepa Textiles. Paint: Benjamin Moore. Laminate: Westinghouse Micarta. Drywall: US Gypsum. Vinyl flooring: VPI. Carpet/carpet tile: Interface. Carbet fibre manufacturer: Monsanto. Ceiling: Armstrong. Lighting: Holophone. Doors: Perkinson Co. Door hardware: Schlage. Glass: McHenry County Glass. Window frames: Northwest Structural Steel. Railings: North-west Structural Steel. Professional desks: Haworth. Professional seating: Haworth. Lounge seating: Vitra; Herman Miller. Upholstery: Haworth; Bernhardt Textiles. Conference tables: Herman Miller. Training tables: Howe. Files: Haworth. Architectural woodwork/cabinet maker: Herner Geissler Woodworking. Steel: North West Structural Steel. Metal: Lundstead Metal. Access flooring: C-Tec Grand Rapids. Furniture dealer: Kayhan International; Thomas Interiors.

Office and Research Centre, Seibersdorf, Austria

Architect and interior design: Coop Himmelb(l)au. Project team: Wolf D. Prix; Helmut Swiczinsky (Partners); Sam; Hopfner; Hornung; Kappus; Mündl; Pillhofer; Spiess; Stojek; Péan; Postl. Client: Austrian Research Centre Seibersdorf. Main contractor: Waagner – Biro (steel construction). Building contractor: Lang and Menhofer. Sub-contractor: Klenk & Meder. Heating and utilities: Bacon. Consultants: Palfinger (measurements); Vasko und Partner (structural engineer); IVAD (ADI I). Façade: Profil Stahl. Exterior glazing: Atmos. Interior glazing: Briza. Water proofing: Haderer, Langenzersdorf. Interior locksmith: Bele Neunkirchen. Drywall, roof: Huber. Paintwork: Berghofer. Tiling: Plattig. Wood floor: Bembe Parkett. Electricity: Klenk & Meder. Interior furnishing: Lazelberger. Joinery: Rehor, Furth. Furnishing: Lista; Kluss. Video: PSV. HVAC: Bacon.

4 CYBERTAINMENT

Philips Fantasy World, Kirchhellen, Bavaria, Germany

Architect and interior design: Matteo Thun. Client: Philips Consumer Electronics. Collaborators: Marco Rossi; Ludolf von Alvensleben. Lighting: Robert Wilson. Furniture and fittings: Lisar Arredamenti SpA. Flooring: Forbo Italia srl. Walls, ceilings and partitions: Koit HighTex GmbH. Illustrator of designs and gadgets: Massimo Giacon.

Planet Hollywood, Walt Disney World, Orlando, Florida, USA

Interior design: Rockwell Architecture Planning and Design PC. Client: Robert Earl, Planet Hollywood International Inc. Main contractor: Welbro Construction. Electrical engineer: Rodin Engineering. Structural engineer: DeSimone, Chaplin & Dobryn. Audio-visual consultant: T. R. Technologies. Kitchen

consultant: Brass & Stainless Designs Inc. Diorama consultant: Modeworks. Lighting: Focus Lighting. Furniture and fittings: Banquettes; A. J. Munitz; ArtCraft. Flooring: US Axminster; Courisan. Glass tiles: Dal-Tile. Textiles: Gilford; J.M. Lynne; Chris Stone; Schumacher.

Café Cyberia, Centre Georges Pompidou, Paris, France

Architect and interior design: Bernhard Blauel Architects. Project team: Bernhard Blauel; Peter Jurschitzka; Miles Layland; Andy Nettleton; Maria Zachariades. Client: Cyberia. Collaborating structural engineer: Brian Lugard; Tom Sammons. Main contractor: Standby Display. M&E: Societe Cegelec. "Cape Pyrok" high-performance structural board: William T. Eden plc. "Expamet" expanded metal: The Expanded Metal Company Ltd. "Metsec" lattice joists: Metsec Building Products. "Flydor" mesh: Flydor Building Products. PVC conduits: Flexicon. "Nomad" cushion plus matting: 3M United Kingdom plc. Linoleum: DLW Linoleum.

Oz City, Tokyo, Japan

Architect: C & A Architects Inc. Designer: Yoshifumi Yamamoto. Client: Escot Corporation. Collaborating designer: Ren Makabe (artwork).

Info Box, Potsdamer Platz, Berlin, Germany

Architects: Schnieder & Schumacher. Project team: Peter Begon; Kristin Dirschl; Petra Pfeiffer; Philipp Schiffer; Christain Simons; Susanne Widmer; Thomas Zürcher. Client: Baustellenlogistik GmbH. Interior design: D & D Kommunikationsdesign. General contractor: Magnus Müller Pinneberg GmbH. Structural engineer: Bollinger & Grohmann. Technical planning: Burckhardt, Emsch & Berger GmbH. Site engineering: Emsch & Berger. Heating and ventilation: Samitär. Lighting: Zumtobel Staff.

Cybersmith, White Plains, Cambridge, Massachusetts, USA

Interior design: Fitch. Project team: Jeff Pacione; Pamela Meada (Art Directors); Pamela Meade; Gideon Ansell; Ed Chung (interface design); Betty Lin; Jean-Andre Villamizar (graphics). Writer: Mike Mooney. Illustrator: Patrick Newberry. Architect: Schwartz Silver. Client: Cybersmith.

Telecom World, Telecom Tower, Hong Kong

Exhibition design: MET Studio. Project team: Alex McCuaig (Art Director); Tim Anderson (Project Manager); Deirdre Janson-Smith (Research Director); Chris White (Senior Researcher); Martin Roche; Alexandra Prescott (Senior Exhibition Designer); Christopher Chesney (Designer); Nick Toft (Architect); Pat O'Leary (Graphics Manager); Helen Rawsthorne (Graphic Designer); Zazu Arnold (a/v specialist). Client: Hongkong Telecom. Main contractor: Wong Ouyang (Building Services) Ltd. Software design: Media Projects International; Graphic Communication Pte Ltd. Audio-visual production: McLean English Associates Video Presentations in the "City Street";

"Just Imagine"; and "Satellite Theatre" exhibits: Lightworks. Supply and co-ordination of hardware and av installations: Electrosonic. Fabrication and installation of exhibits: Maltbie Associates. Lighting: DHA Design.

Futurevision: This is Tomorrow, Manchester, UK
Interior exhibition design; John Csaky: Button/Csaky. Project team: John Csaky (Project Director); Richard Diamond (Project Co-ordination); David Cogswell (Exhibition Design); Sally Conran; Karl AbeyKasekera. Client: Granada. Main contractor: Melville Exhibition and Museum Ltd. Illuminations: AV Software. AV hardware system: Electrosonic Ltd. Graphics: Atoll Ltd. Lighting design: Sutton-Vane Associates. Cost management: Ian Symonds Associates. M & E and structural engineers: Buro Happold, Consulting Engineers.

Virtual World Center, Pasadena, California, USA
Architect and interior design: Pica & Sullivan architects Ltd. Project team: V. Joseph Pica (Project Designer); Maureen Sullivan (Principal-in-Charge); Serena Yee Winner (Project Architect); Steve Klauner; Helen Pietrusiewicz (interiors); Lisa Oliveri Carroll (interiors). Client: Virtual World Entertainment Inc. Main contractor: Fisher Development Inc. Collaborators: Shelton Design (specialized furniture designs); Englekirk & Sabol, Inc. (structural engineers); The Sullivan Partnership (mechanical engineering); Kanwar and Associates (electrical engineering); California Restaurant Contractors Inc. (kitchen design); Purchase Planners Inc. (furniture consultant). Lighting: American Wholesale Lighting. Custom furniture: Shelton Design. Furniture: Purchase Planners Group. Custom carpet: Contract Distributors Corporation. Drapes: Richard Williams. Custom wallcovering: Thybony. Props: Dawne Weisman. Scenic painting: Specer Davis. Custom casework: Royston Inc.

Trocadero Renovation, London, UK
Interior architects: RTKL-UK Ltd. Client: Burford Group plc. Project management: Mace. Show consultant: Media Projects. Audio-visual consultant: Vincent Rice: Design. Lighting consultant: Jonathan Speirs & Associates.

Segaworld Theme Park, London, UK
Architects and design consultants: Tibbatts Associates. Client: Sega Amusements Europe Ltd. Collaborators: John Nolan Associates (engineers); Bucknall Austin (quantity surveyors); Mace (construction managers). Setwork contractors: T.H.E. (Themes, Heritage & Exhibitions Ltd) Level 6, Segaworld reception and combat zone; Terrance Dickson Associates Ltd (Level 4, the race track and flight deck); Kimpton Walker (Level 3, the carnival; Level 2, the sports arena, queue lines and certain rides). Flooring: Forbo Nairn Ltd (supplier); A1 Flooring Ltd (installation). Sculptures: Michael Whiteley Associates Ltd.

5 KNOWLEDGE EXCHANGES

Main Public Library, San Francisco, California, USA
Architect and interior design: Pei Cobb Freed & Partners.

Project team: James Ingo Freed (Partner/Design); Werner Wandelmaier (Partner/Management); Michael D. Flynn (Partner/Technology/Management); Lloyds G. Ware (Associate Partner/Management); Christopher L. Olsen (Senior Associate/Curtain Wall); Jennifer Sage (Senior Associate/Design); Robert Madey (Senior Associate/Design Management); Kyle Johnson (Senior Associate/Construction Administration); Richard Gorman (Senior Associate/Specifications); Kirk Conover (Associate/Design and Construction Documents); Nancy Sun (Associate/Skylights and Roof); Gianni Neri (Associate/Construction Administration); Eric Cugnart; Ali Gidfar; Kevin Johns; Ramin Rezai; Sandra Lutes; Mercedes Stadthagen; Mark Hill; Shadi Nazarian; Felecia Davis; Patricia Lubary; William Lee; John Lee; Hotae Kang; Sara Rose; Jennifer Adler; Frank Starkey; Oreste Drapaca; Carol Averill; Michelle Transou; Marc Drapau. Client: City and County of San Francisco. Associate architect and interior design: Simon Martin-Vegue Winkelstein Moris. Interior design: Kwan Henmi. Main contractor: Huber, Hunt & Nichols Inc. Construction manager: Bureau of Construction Management in conjunction with O'Brian Kreitzberg & Associates. Structural consultant: OLMM Structural Design. Base isolation: Forell/Elesser Engineers Inc. Mechanical/electrical/plumbing/telecommunications: Flack & Kurtz; SJ Engineers; Peter O. Lapid & Associates. Fire/life safety: Rolf Jensen Associates; A. R. Sanchez-Corea. Lighting: Fisher Marantz Renfro Stone, Inc.; ALD/David Malman. Elevators: Hesselberg, Keesee & Associates. Audio-visual/acoustical consultants: Paoletti Associates Inc. Civil engineers: F. E. Jordan Associates Inc. Landscape: Carter Tighe Leeming & Kajiwara. Graphics: X (+C) Ltd; Studio A. (children's library). Roofing: Lance Roof Inspection Service Inc. Exterior building maintenance: Lerch, Bates & Associates. Hardware: Bruce Purdy. Ventilation: Hal Levin & Associates. Specifications: John Raeber. Costing: Adamson Associates; Oppenheim, Lewis Inc. Colour: Donald Kaufman. Artists: Alice Aycock (Functional and Fantasy Stair and Cyclone Fragment in the periodicals room); Nayland Blake (constellation in monumental stairway – lighting by Nayland Blake); Ann Hamilton and Ann Chamberlain (untitled installation on diagonal wall); Charley Brown and Mark Evans (Into the Light – ceiling of Gay and Lesbian Centre).

Media Park, Ichikawa, Japan
Architect and interior design: Yamashita Sekkei Inc. Project team: Takeshi Hashimoto & Toshiya Yasuda. Client: Ichikawa-City. Collaborator: Shinji Tomie (library consultant). Main contractor: Takenaka; Kamijo. Lighting: Yamagiwa Corporation. Furniture and fittings: Okamura Corporation. Brickwork: Takayama Engineering Inc.

University of Cambridge Law Faculty, Cambridge, UK
Architect: Sir Norman Foster and Partners. Project team: Norman Foster; Spencer de Grey; John Silver; Chris Connell; Michael Jones; Mouzhan Majidi; Giuseppe Boscherini; Angus Campbell; Glenis Fan; Jason Flanagan; Lucy Highton; Ben Marshall; Divya Patel; Kate Peake; Victoria Pike; Austin Relton; Giles Robinson; John Small; Ken Wai; Cindy Walters; Ricarda

Zimmerer. Client: University of Cambridge. Project management: University of Cambridge, Estates Management and Building Services. Main contractor: Taylor Wodrow Construction. Clerk of Works: Andrew Merrick. Quantity surveyor: Davis Langdon & Everest. Structural engineer: Anthony Hunt Associates. Services engineer: YRM Engineers. Acoustic consultant: Sandy Brown Associates. Cladding consultant: Emmer Pfenniger Partner AG. Fire engineer: Ove Arup & Partners. Concrete frame: Duffy Construction. Precast concrete: Malling Precast. Structural steelwork: Westbury Tubular Structures. External cladding: Metalbau Früh (UK). Mechanical and electrical services: Drake and Scull Engineering. Ground works: Hiretest. Suspended metal ceilings and roof linings: Entech. Lighting: Erco. Glazed overpanels, glass partitions and floor: Solaglas. Atrium staircase and glazed balustrade: Hubbard Architectural Metalwork. Steel escape staircase: Weland. Granite floors and wall: Stonecase. Timber wall panelling: FR Shadbolt and Sons. Carpet: Tyndale Carpets; Ulster Carpets. Fixed library shelving: Acerbis International. Compact library shelving: Electrolux Bruynzeel. Auditorium seating: Race Upholstery. Reception desk and furniture: Tecno. Wall storage system: Dancontract. Loose furniture and café tables: Aram Design. JCR bar: Tam Engineering. JCR benches: Malling Precast. Internal timber doors: Jandor. Ironmongery: Elementer. Stainless steel servery and catering equipment: Gratte Brothers. Roller shutters: Bolton Brady. External grilles and architectural metalwork: Robinson Metalwork. Audio-visual equipment: Metro Video. Lifts: Express Lifts. Raised floors: Halfen Unistrut.

Bibliothèque Nationale de France, Paris, France
Architect and interior design: Perrault Architecte. Project team: Dominique Perrault; Daniel Allaire; Gabriel Choukroun; Guy Morisseau; Yves Conan; Constantin Coursaris; Maxime Gasperini; Pable Gil; Luciano d'Alesio; Claude Alovisetti; Emmanuelle Andréani; Judith Barber; Phlippe Berbett; Jérôme Besse; Jean-Luc Bichet; Charles Caglini; Jean-François Candeille; Hristo Chinkov; Alexander Dierendonck; Céline Dos Santos; Marie-France Dussaussois; Laura Ferreira-Sheehan; Corrina Fuhrer; Catriona Gatheral; Dominique Guibert; Serge Guyon; Dominique Jauvin; Anne Kaplan; Christian Laborde; Maryvonne Lanco; Corinne Lafon; Olivier Lidon; Zhi-Jian Lin; Pierre Loritte; Patrice Marchand; Thierry Meunier; Brigitte Michaud; Franck Michigan; Rosa Precigout; René Puybonnieux; Martine Rigaud; Hildegard Ruske; Jérôme Thibault; Catherine Todaro; Louis van Ost; Inge Waes. Client: Bibliothèque Nationale de France. Project management: Socotec. Project control: ODM. Lighting and acoustics: Jean-Paul Lamoureux. Tropical forest technical centre: CTFT. Structural engineer: Sechaud & Bossuyt. Electrical engineer: GTME. Climatic engineering: Danto Rogeat. Lifts: Otis. Woodwork and metalwork: Construction bois Baumert; Jacqmin. Landscape design: Sauveterre-Horizon. Tree planting: SNMV. Scenography: Didier Onde/Sophie Thomas. Interiors: Dennery (350-seat conference area, north/south reading rooms); Bel SA (lecture, research and public east/west reading rooms); Ateliers Normand (200-seat conference room); SPR Entreprise (reception and personnel

restaurant); Bredy SA (public reading rooms). Lighting: Zumtobel Staff. Suppliers: Sibt (wood); Mazda (external lighting); Sammode (internal lighting).

Universität II, Ulm, Germany
Architect and project direction: Steidle and Partner. Project team: Otto Steidle; Siegwart Geiger; Alexander Lux; Peter Schmitz; Johann Spengler; Ralf Rasch; Colette Almesberger; Toni Leismüller. Project management: Siegfried Kowanda; Manfred Teubner; Peter Freese, Christina Hïgerl. Client: Ulm University. Structural engineers: Sailer-Stepan-Bloos. Colour: Erich Wiesner. Landscaping: Peter Latz & Partner.

Phoenix Central Library, Phoenix, Arizona, USA
Architect and interior design: Bruder DWL Architects – William P. Bruder. Planners: DWL Architects & Planners. Project team: Will Bruder; Wendell Burnette (lead designers); Carleton Van Deman (Project Manager); Bob Adams; Marc Arnold; Lito Aquino; Maryann Bloomfield; John Chopas; Lauren Clark; Mark Dee; Beau Dormiach; Dan Filuk; Micheal Haake; Frank Henry, Toni Ann Hindlye; Sharon Kraus; Rick Joy; James Lindlan; Dean Olsen; Peter Pascu; Vicky Kamella; Jeff Wagner. Client: City of Phoenix. Main contractor: Sundt Corp. Engineer: Ove Arup & Partner (structural/acoustic/building systems); Bates/Valentino Associates (building systems); Hook Engineering (civil). Consultants: Mason Associates, Professional Library Consultants (library); Lighting Dynamics (lighting); Tait Solar Company (daylighting); Construction Consultants Southwest (costing); FTL/Happold (structural fabric). Lighting: Zumtobel Staff.

Newman Library and Technology Center, Baruch College of The City University of New York, New York, USA
Architect and interior design: Davis, Brody & Associates, LLP. Client: Baruch College of the City University of New York. Main contractor: Morse Diesel. Structural engineer: Ewell W. Finley PC. MEP engineers: Syska & Hennesy Inc. Lighting design: Fisher, Marantz, Renfro, Stone.

Ueda City Multimedia Information Centre, Ueda, Japan
Architect and interior design: Project Development Division, Dentsu Inc. Project team: Matsumi Ishikawa (building and exhibition systems); Izumi Hiroshi (images and software). Client: Ueda City. Collaborating Architect: Akira Komiyama (unity architecture and planning).

Science, Industry and Business Library (SIBL), The New York Public Library, New York, USA
Architect and interior design: Gwathmey Siegel & Associates Architects. Project team: Charles Gwathmey; Robert Siegel (Principals-in-Charge); Jacob Alspector (Associate-in-Charge); Earl Swisher (Project Architect); Sean Flynn (Project Direction); Karen Brenner; Oana Bretcanu; Wendy Burger; Federico Del Priore; Seven Forman; Mike Harshman; Philip Henshaw; Mark Hill; Rebecca Iovino; John Johnston; James Leet; Martin Marciano;David Mateer; Cheryl McQueen; Mark Montalbano;Jeffrey Poorten (Construction Administration); Joseph Rivera; Elizabeth Skowronek; Tom Levering (Competition); Joseph Ruocco (Master Plan). Client: New York Public Library. Construction manager: AJ Contracting Company Inc. Structural engineers: Severud Associates. Electro/mechanical engineers: Jaros Baum & Bolles. A/V consultant. Shen Milsom and Wilke. Graphics/signage consultant: Spagnola & Associates. Electronic display consultant: Edwin Schlossberg Inc. Elevator consultant: Jaros Baum & Bolles. Furniture consultant: Hillman Di Bernardo & Assoc. Inc. Security consultant: Chapman Ducibella Associates. Specifications: Specifications Associates Inc. Telecom consultant: DVI Communications Inc.

INDEX OF ARCHITECTS, DESIGNERS AND PROJECTS